| ..NDLES

Iain Landles

WAR TRILOGY

THE SIEGE
ANGEL OF MONS
BEREZINA

OBERON BOOKS
LONDON

First published in 2005 by Oberon Books Ltd
521 Caledonian Road, London N7 9RH
Tel: 020 7607 3637 / Fax: 020 7607 3629
e-mail: oberon.books@btinternet.com
www.oberonbooks.com

A catalogue record for this book is available from the British
Library.

ISBN: 1 84002 543 3

Cover by Scott Suttey

Printed in Great Britain by Antony Rowe Ltd, Chippenham

Contents

THE SIEGE, 11

ANGEL OF MONS, 83

BEREZINA, 147

Some had to do with *the art of theatre*, but finding it too arduous, chose to join *the theatre.* These are legion. A few remained faithful. Very few, because it is a painful path.

Howard Barker, *Death, The One and the Art of Theatre*

For Jo

THE SIEGE

Characters

JOSEPH

ANNA

HENRI

SIMON

LASCARIS

TONI

MARIA

LUCY

BERNARD

'VOICE'

SOLDIERS

TURKS

The Siege was first performed by Concussion Productions at the White Bear Theatre, London, on Tuesday 16 September 2003, with the following cast:

JOSEPH, Tunde Makinde

ANNA, Kathleen Kimi

HENRI, Graham Slayford

SIMON, Tom Woodman

LASCARIS, Mark Healey

TONI, Gareth Parker

MARIA, Lucy Fredrick

LUCY, Kirsty Wills

'VOICE' / BERNARD / TURK / SOLDIER,
James Klienmann

TURK / SOLDIER, James Jeffrey

Directed by Vincent Adams

ACT ONE

Scene One

A chamber high above the city of Valletta, Malta. Light cascades through tall windows, throwing beams of light across the floor. Present are HENRI DE LA VALLETTE, LASCARIS, JOSEPH, and TONI. HENRI stares out of one of the windows. From below a tumult of noise as the Siege of Malta continues.

HENRI: I heard the voice of the fourth beast say, Come
and see.
And I looked, and behold a pale horse:
And his name that sat on him was Death,
And Hell followed with him.
And power was given unto them over the fourth part of
the earth,
To kill with sword,
And with hunger,
And with death...
Bollocks to that.
Do you think Death is a personification, Lascaris?

LASCARIS: We are all death –

HENRI: **A straight answer wouldn't go amiss here.** I
mean, if Death is a personification, does he shit?

LASCARIS: Such irreverence –

HENRI: Shut up –

LASCARIS: When men are being slaughtered –

HENRI: Enough –

LASCARIS: I find disgusting –

HENRI: Oh, shut up –

LASCARIS: And degrading to –

HENRI: **Know it –**

LASCARIS: Then why the fuck –

HENRI: I'm the boss here and if... Abstraction. A way of
dealing with... I mean, accepting the large... **For fuck
sakes you know what I mean**

LASCARIS: You ponder and another fifty men die –

HENRI: **Know that!** Why aren't you in charge, Lascaris?

LASCARIS: Like to kill not…ponder.

HENRI: (*Laughs.*) I see the problem – intellectualism is the curse of happiness. Look at them these rutting, killing, banal…things! Hardly people; not in the sense that we know. No. Beasts. Slobbering beasts intent on pleasure and mayhem. And in their dumbness they find happiness. Whilst we intellectuals –

LASCARIS: You are not an intellectual. You can barely read. If the truth be known, I rewrite your orders to make them intelligible.

HENRI: I know that – **don't think I don't know that!** So, you are in charge after all!

LASCARIS: Must we, every day, go through this façade…

HENRI: Therefore shall her plagues come in one day, death, and –

LASCARIS: I know –

HENRI: Mourning, and famine; and she shall be utterly burned with fire:

LASCARIS: **Know it –**

HENRI: For strong is the Lord God who judgeth her –

LASCARIS: Another fifty perish –

HENRI: If we are the righteous –

LASCARIS: **Shut up!** So you want to hear again just how great you are. Henri the brave; the valiant. Only Henri can stem the evil Muslim tide. His cunning and his strength of purpose. Would you, at this point, care to listen to the testimonies? Exactly how the men love you? Or how the locals revere you? They say you are a saint! There! It's been said. Now can we get the fuck on?

HENRI: A saint? Really?

LASCARIS: For fuck's sake…

HENRI: Tell them that I am honoured, that…

(*HENRI stops and trembles violently. LASCARIS grabs HENRI and holds him. HENRI looks up into LASCARIS' eyes. A passage of time.*)

Do you hate me, Lascaris?

LASCARIS: You know I do.

HENRI: (*Pushing LASCARIS off.*) Surrounded by truth. No shelter in manners. Joseph, am I a saint to you?

JOSEPH: That is blasphemy, irrelevant, non-military, and tiresome.

HENRI: You think I procrastinate?

JOSEPH: We just want the daily orders, sire. The rantings, the ravings, the mock religious tone – all designed to frustrate. Yes, you procrastinate, but do so without clear purpose. You must, as you do every day, eventually face the situation. When you do, when we have endured much, then you will come to your senses and issue the orders.

HENRI: You hate me too?

JOSEPH: No, my lord. Without you the Turks would have destroyed us. Genius must out.

HENRI: If only I knew what the fuck you were talking about –

LASCARIS: The men on the East wall haven't been relieved in three weeks –

HENRI: Boring –

LASCARIS: The central garrison hasn't sufficient weaponry to repulse any sort of attack –

HENRI: Know it –

LASCARIS: The locals starve. They may turn against us –

HENRI: **Know it** –

LASCARIS: The Turks breached the South wall last night; we repelled the attack, but at huge cost. Captain Steiner was lost.

HENRI: Steiner? How...terrible. I must write to his wife. She once said how beautiful my eyes were. She told me, in confidence, how all she wanted was a child with Steiner, and now... **I smelt spunk from her loins** –

LASCARIS: There is no word from the Vatican. What are you orders?

HENRI: When they die – do they – I mean – do they – what must they – words – if only I had the fucking words –

17

(*SIMON, with assembled entourage, enters with a flourish of activity.*)

SIMON: Sire! How you glow with vitality! If I'm not mistaken you wear the jasmine scent I gave you! See? I knew it would suit you! Trust me on these matters, sire, image is all in times as these. Henri de La Vallette is more than a god-warrior – he also is the best dressed man in the Mediterranean! Please, pass out these invitations, I mean, in these times social gatherings at least blunt the reality.

HENRI: Lascaris would like to rip your throat out.

SIMON: He would like to rip everyone's throat out! But that is why we admire him.

HENRI: He thinks you superficial and vulgar.

SIMON: My best qualities! (*Laughter.*) Lascaris, did the balm work?

LASCARIS: I, er...well –

HENRI: Balm? What balm?

SIMON: Lascaris may be the most savage of soldiers, but even his arse gets sore from time to time.

(*Laughter, to which even LASCARIS joins in. JOSEPH glares at SIMON.*)

I mean it is an ill wind that blows no good – and you said it was the dog! (*More laughter.*) But come, my dear friends, we all serve as best we can. You fight for us, and the Holy Roman Empire, but after the fighting, merchants like me will rebuild what war has torn asunder.

LASCARIS: Sire, the orders.

HENRI: You should be here more often, Simon. You presence cheers up our angry Lascaris.

SIMON: You do me the greatest honour, sire.

HENRI: Well then, let us proceed –

JOSEPH: Pardon, sire, but Simon Bulbous is still present.

SIMON: Such a crime? I too have news of importance; news that may well affect the daily orders. I am important despite contrary to appearances. Let's be honest, appearances is my best suit. (*Laughter.*) Anyhow, Henri has invited me to this and all future meetings.

JOSEPH: This is true, sire?

HENRI: What of it?

JOSEPH: He is non-military.

SIMON: True but I throw the best parties! Now, if we had dancing girls and a little to smoke...
(*There is laughter. JOSEPH stares at SIMON.*)
However, I bring this meeting news of a rebellious plot among the locals –

JOSEPH: I have heard no such thing –

SIMON: With respect, Joseph, maybe you spend too much time looking outward and not enough time looking inward –

JOSEPH: And you may well spend a lot of time looking at my sword as I ram it down your throat –

HENRI: **If you two are gonna bicker** –

SIMON: Apologies, sire.

HENRI: What is wrong with these people? We come here to save their puny island against the might of the Turks and all they do is moan!

SIMON: It's about food, sire.

HENRI: What of it?

SIMON: They have none.

HENRI: Technicalities –

SIMON: True, but ignore them and they will fuck you.

HENRI: Well put.

JOSEPH: All lies –

LASCARIS: Joseph –

HENRI: Maybe not –

JOSEPH: Oh, come on –

SIMON: The human factor –

JOSEPH: The man lies –

LASCARIS: Enough!

SIMON: Cannot ignore the locals –

JOSEPH: Dismiss him –

SIMON: To do so is suicide –

JOSEPH: Rip his lying tongue out –

LASCARIS: Joseph –

JOSEPH: Ram skewers into his eyes –

HENRI: **Joseph –**

JOSEPH: **He swans around like a –**

SIMON: And I know how to deal with it.

(*A pause of contemplation.*)

HENRI: Well?

SIMON: I have made contact with people who could, at a price, help –

JOSEPH: You see the deceiver he really is?

SIMON: Smuggle in, at great cost to themselves –

JOSEPH: **Stamp out this vermin!**

LASCARIS: (*To JOSEPH.*) If you say one more word…

SIMON: We could reverse the situation –

(*JOSEPH starts to speak.*)

HENRI: No, Joseph! **Quiet!** I am the genius here. It's what I'm paid for. Remember that. A superficial, arrogant runt he may be, but all the same, we deal with him. Understood?

JOSEPH: My lord.

SIMON: Can I use that as a character reference, sire?

(*Laughter.*)

HENRI: Lascaris?

LASCARIS: It is possible, sire. The atmosphere on the streets is tense. The locals may well be up to something.

HENRI: Whatever he wants, give him. See to it, Lascaris. Good-looking swines such as him always get what they want eventually.

JOSEPH: **At what cost?**

LASCARIS: **I'm gonna fuck you in a minute.**

HENRI: Spare the insights, Joseph. Remember your rank in this room. Do it.

(*LASCARIS bows and exits with JOSEPH.*)

SIMON: My lord –

HENRI: **Don't!** Go.

(*SIMON bows and exits with entourage.*)

How did I do?

TONI: Better, but I would forget the bible quotes.

HENRI: It didn't add a touch of authority?

TONI: More a touch of banality.

HENRI: If only I had Simon's touch. Life and soul.

TONI: Still.

HENRI: I sometimes...the... I mean...all these people... As if the slightest snowflake would send them to the dark –

TONI: Still.

HENRI: I dream...such things –

TONI: Know it –

HENRI: And her face and noisecoloured eyes –

TONI: **Know it** –

(*HENRI begins to undo his shirt and takes it off.*)

HENRI: If there was green here...**inflections of solace**...all tremble –

TONI: Still.

HENRI: Always the same...always the same...seems the stars are torn –

TONI: Still.

(*TONI exits but returns quickly carrying a small lit candle.*)

HENRI: And the sea gave up the dead which were in it –

TONI: Down.

HENRI: And death and hell delivered up the dead which were in them –

TONI: **Down.**

(*HENRI falls to his knees and bends slightly forward. TONI begins to drip the hot candle wax onto HENRI's back. HENRI gasps in pain.*)

HENRI: And they were judged –

(*TONI drips more wax onto HENRI.*)

Every man according to their works –

(*More.*)

And death and hell were cast into the lake of fire –

(*More.*)

This is the second death...

(*The scene ends to the sound of HENRI's pain.*)

Scene Two

A church. ANNA sits in the gloom. JOSEPH enters, crosses himself, and kneels to pray. A silence.

ANNA: Sleep on the floor?

JOSEPH: (*Startled.*) What…?

ANNA: Yon rusty stuff holding you together.

JOSEPH: God's armour.

ANNA: No slogans in the sanctuary sleep in it? On the floor?

JOSEPH: My back is shattered –

ANNA: My husband has a small cock –

JOSEPH: Madam –

ANNA: Small cock yet still climbs aboard panting pawing beast feasting –

JOSEPH: I think –

ANNA: He pleads with me as I lay frigid-cold what to do? How to touch? He sobs what do you like?

JOSEPH: Please –

ANNA: A huge stomach – small cock huge stomach a prick in a haystack –

JOSEPH: I –

ANNA: I tell you all this because you are a knight of God –

JOSEPH: Am no confessor –

ANNA: All the same…you eat?

JOSEPH: As well as –

ANNA: Skin and bones wrapped in rust I dream of roasting lamb turning with bubbling juices spit-spat-hiss turning-turning-turning glistening in the dream light –

JOSEPH: Futile to –

ANNA: But the cooks won't stop turning-turning-turning and all is burnt tastes of ashes wake to ashes in the mouth –

JOSEPH: The Turks burn all the trees, seems as if desolation descends upon us.

ANNA: You knights of God glow in the brilliance of innocence yet stained with visions of the void –

JOSEPH: Never –

ANNA: Is it not true that you Knights of God loot? Burn? Maim? Rape?

JOSEPH: Some are guilty –

ANNA: All are guilty of something. Do they wear the cross when fucking some Muslim girl?

JOSEPH: I don't –

ANNA: Red cross splashed with red blood teach me the subtlety of shades –

JOSEPH: Not perfect. To seek perfection is the aim –

ANNA: Doing God's work with your cock up some Muslim's arse. Which psalm was that in?

JOSEPH: So hard – you would break at the faintest touch.

ANNA: Hard? It comes from living with an animal. No, not animal something not human –

JOSEPH: I believe you are the worst liar I have known.

ANNA: You...

JOSEPH: Lies hang off you like cheap jewellery.

ANNA: I fight insidious wars no limits to what we suffer what we inflict no final victory just tactics, evasions, trickery, lies.

JOSEPH: Then why –

ANNA: To punish to hurt to mutilate – the ultimate love. Don't you do this in the name of God? Slaughtering Muslims?

JOSEPH: The heathen barbarians, yes –

ANNA: An expert! You have of course examined the barbarians' culture? How they enslave children rape women to impregnate them with the next generation of swine how they mutilate enemies carving obscene curses on bleached dead skin.

JOSEPH: I have heard of such things.

ANNA: (*Laughs.*) Know nothing! Not the mullah's prays in the twilight the haunting strains of troubadour's singing of loss – they come not to burn pictures rape women how could they? Would you die for a painting? A woman? No, not yet. They do as you do both led by the nose man's accustomed position.

JOSEPH: It is a duty to God to defend the faith –

ANNA: How strong this bastion? In the babble of murder who stops to think? A spectrum of corpses in waiting each with a reason to hate –

JOSEPH: Duty to God –

ANNA: (*Laughs.*) My children play in a small garden high above the city. There the air is keen and the sun tumbles as caresses. Amid the perfume and colours they laugh. Even the pounding rhythms of guns become play. Amid the carnage laughter of angels floats down and sometimes men stop to listen. I watch. How they listen. And as tears flow from red eyes they renew the slaughter. That's all. They fight to hear angels laugh. Not God. Duty. You bring that. And of course to fuck their wives in peace –

JOSEPH: Your baseness grinds –

ANNA: So what! What's wrong with baseness?

JOSEPH: Our duty to keep control –

ANNA: I bet your cock is massive –

JOSEPH: Please!

ANNA: Huge skin and bones but colossal cock –

JOSEPH: I must warn you –

ANNA: Are you celibate? They say the Knights of God shy away from female flesh – those who aren't fucking at the time –

JOSEPH: I took the oath.

ANNA: And duty –

JOSEPH: Dictates I remain pure. God's reward is all I seek.

ANNA: So you've never fucked –

JOSEPH: I cannot listen to –

ANNA: Wait! (*ANNA moves closer and looks into his eyes.*) I see pain lines how the seasons have burnt and cracked your skin the paths you have trodden the annihilated lands of waste only your eyes float soft see how they ask. (*She stares into his eyes. Suddenly she slaps him.*) Your eyes ask...and you a Knight of God!

JOSEPH: (*Confused.*) I...but –

ANNA: (*Darts in close to JOSEPH and kisses him on the cheek.*) I mock forgive forgive.

JOSEPH: My Lady's wit is, I am afraid, beyond my
    meagre –

ANNA: No humour! Didn't Jesus ever smile?

JOSEPH: There is no evidence –

ANNA: What are you afraid of?
    (*Pause.*)

JOSEPH: The loss of God…

ANNA: You have already lost him –

JOSEPH: No!

ANNA: One can see it in you. Your body. Your face.
    Absence of god.

JOSEPH: In the last campaign a scorched and arid place a
    terribly afar land I rested beside a road watching an alien
    twilight steal forth to murder the day strange lonely
    birds cried out again and again and in parched blasted
    rocks strangled flowers of dust spread their noxious
    stench in this cacophony of brutality a soldier of my
    troop spotted a rat and with nauseous rapidity stomped
    his boot down upon it squashing its back legs and
    bursting open its stomach yet still it lived using its front
    legs to crawl towards its hole the men gathered around
    to observe its plight as it heaved and gasped crawling
    inch by terrifying inch dirt and sand sticking to its
    insides and swarms of furious flies feeding upon its
    lifeblood and being unable to listen to its wheezing and
    frantic shrill screams I stood up and stamped upon its
    head until it moved no more…

ANNA: And you think this shows an absence of God?

JOSEPH: I know only that I feel more for the rat than the
    thousands of butchered souls I have seen murdered
    before me.

ANNA: You are a beautiful man all the same you will die
    horribly and the Turks will cut off your massive cock
    and shove it into your mouth –

JOSEPH: Again she –

ANNA: Even before that you must suffer –

JOSEPH: Suffer?

ANNA: (*Suddenly holds JOSEPH's head in her hands.*) I shall
    replace your God and you shall follow me my merest
    breath your only concern my slightest look your
    obsession and you shall be my dog yapping after me
    snivelling when I ignore you performing tricks only to
    please me and when the mood suits I will throw you
    scraps of attention and this will be your heart's desire
    forever and ever amen.
    (*ANNA exits. JOSEPH stands in a daze for a while before
    sinking to his knees.*)

Scene Three

*SIMON's chamber. Attendants wait on SIMON, who browses through
paperwork. A girl, MARIA, sits on a sofa. The siege is heard distantly.*

SIMON: No, no. Tell Michaels that the aim isn't to extort
    money from the people. Prices must be kept stable
    otherwise our monopoly will collapse. Tell him to charge
    exactly what I stipulated and no more. Greed is not the
    point here. Time enough for that. Planning and
    execution – they are the key words. Keep a watch on
    him.
    (*An attendant leaves.*)
    Distribute free water to the soldiers on the North wall.
    Tell the commander there that it is a present from me to
    him in recognition of the valour of his men. I don't want
    his thanks just his presence at dinner tomorrow evening.
    (*An attendant leaves.*)
MARIA: St Christopher's Street burns –
SIMON: It always does –
MARIA: People starve –
SIMON: Not for long –
MARIA: You promised me lace –
SIMON: And you will get it. Everyone will get what they
    deserve –
MARIA: French lace, not that crap Spanish stuff –
SIMON: Of course, would I allow my dear Maria to wear
    Spanish lace?

THE SIEGE: ACT ONE

MARIA: Your wife receives the most exquisite things –
(*SIMON begins to smoke from a pipe and occasionally the smoke takes away his breath.*)

SIMON: You misunderstand love –

MARIA: You love her?

SIMON: As I do my right arm. Ordinarily it hardly exists for me...but if I lost it...how would I wipe my arse?

MARIA: A possession –

SIMON: Oh, no. We inhabit each other. Beyond words. Beyond love.

MARIA: Then why fuck me?

SIMON: (*Laughs.*) The mere act of fucking is just the depositing of two ounces of slime. An overrated activity. You women honestly think that you have something special between your legs –

MARIA: You thought so once –

SIMON: I've seen women sold for a loaf of bread – half a loaf! Parading themselves – opening their legs with the spunk of others still dribbling from their rancid holes – **what's so special 'bout that?**

MARIA: There can be love, without which **do you tell her you love her?**

SIMON: My continued presence is enough. Words fail at the edge of things. But you...if life with me is so bad...why stay? Do I wrong you in any way? Beat you? Threaten you? No. So, why?

MARIA: Duty –

SIMON: Ahh –

MARIA: Only I know what you need. How to treat you. What you like –

SIMON: That is –

MARIA: **Obsession! What's wrong with that!**

SIMON: Nothing. Despise those who tell you different. Without you what am I?

MARIA: We have our love, only it's a new kind of love.

SIMON: I tell you, I could do...such things! Ambition and drive and energy and the money! The power! Who knows the limits! And at the end, only by you my heart always beats.

MARIA: Me?

SIMON: Like this hemp – a delicacy of sensation. Pleasure. Pleasure brings its own depths.

MARIA: And no more?

SIMON: For what purpose? Pain? The world tilts…crazily jagged planes clash – serrating lines and in the screaming we tumble from one hurt to another. Stability, for all its suffocation, can be a valuable commodity.

MARIA: In dawn's murky palate I stir and the profoundest thoughts with my mind play and such thoughts hushed as midnight snow drifting thus and ever and –

SIMON: You fart like a donkey in the morning.

MARIA: Why don't you touch me anymore?

(*SIMON ignores her and smokes.*)

I worry at your latest plan.

(*SIMON smokes.*)

To watch others fuck me.

(*SIMON smokes.*)

The basest, filthiest disease-ridden scum – fucking me.

(*SIMON smokes.*)

Using me. Pawing my flesh. Gripping and pulling. Their sweat smearing my perfection. Their cum staining my purity.

(*SIMON smokes.*)

And you wish to lick up their mess.

(*SIMON smokes.*)

You. You abase yourself – licking their mess – fumbling to be erect – frustrated diamond tears – and you mock my cunt –

SIMON: Friends approach. Influential friends. I will fawn you will smile. I will ingratiate you will smile. I will bow and scrape you will smile.

MARIA: What friends?

SIMON: Only smile.

(*A silence where SIMON smokes. They stare at each other. Presently three TURKS enter. The TURKS regard SIMON with open hostility. He notices them and smiles broadly, suddenly animated.*)

Gentlemen, may Allah –

TURK 1: No pleasantries – you, Christian, are a prick.
Forget that not.

SIMON: Then you honour me, for aren't they, at least,
useful?

TURK 1: Her?

SIMON: A bauble, nothing more.

(*MARIA smiles.*)

Please, be seated.

TURK 1: No.

SIMON: How boring. Still. Shall we play a game?

TURK 1: No time for childish games –

SIMON: Oh, what does it matter? What's your problem?
Time enough for seriousness.

TURK 1: Mocking us –

SIMON: Come on. I know! Let's take off our pants!

(*SIMON pulls down his pants. The TURKS stand agog.
MARIA giggles.*)

You next!

TURK 3: Let me kill him –

SIMON: Perhaps the winner of the game gets the reward.

(*Much silence.*)

TURK 2: Of what?

SIMON: Who knows? Perhaps a silver coin. As much fruit
as you can eat. A holiday! A ride on a camel with your
best friend –

TURK 3: I will kill him –

SIMON: Or even the weak spots of our defences…

(*Much soul searching from the TURKS. A final, unspoken
agreement.*)

TURK 2: What…exactly are the…rules of this…game?

SIMON: That's the spirit! We all take off our pants!

(*The TURKS, stunned and angry, pull off their pants. MARIA
giggles furiously. The TURKS glare at her.*)

Shall we wank?

TURK 1: Enough!

SIMON: Perhaps not. Maria…stand.

(*MARIA, sensing danger, slowly stands.*)

Now...strip.

MARIA: Simon –

SIMON: **Strip!**

(*MARIA strips naked. The TURKS stare.*)

Now, gentlemen. Let us play.

MARIA: Simon, please –

TURK 2: What...exactly are the...rules to this...game?

SIMON: Dunno. Let us see who can come up with the most...novel...humiliation...

(*MARIA turns to run but is quickly caught by TURK 1. The TURKS gather around MARIA and pull her, screaming, to the ground. SIMON watches and moves closer to get a better view.*)

And don't come in her! Come on her! The first gets the prize! I am the judge! I am the judge!

(*The lights snap out with MARIA's scream.*)

Scene Four

HENRI's chamber. The siege is heard distantly.

HENRI: Twisted...ribbons of...streaming...and slime as if...such bluecold, imagine that, in this heat...the stench of darkness...raining down, the kiss of death, raining down...but their faces...such beauty in those faces...oh, yes, they talked to me – why not?

JOSEPH: The dead?

HENRI: Yes, yes. **You think the living have the monopoly on language?** Of course, they weren't exactly fluent. No, more...stumbling...grotesque stumbling. Like an awful pain awakening.

JOSEPH: My Lord, they were merely death rattles –

HENRI: Death does not rattle! It shrieks and bellows a dissonance of wailing. I have heard ... such sounds ...

JOSEPH: The battlefield is a charnel house –

HENRI: Poetry, all the same. If we readily embrace the beauty, then we must also embrace the ugly.

(*HENRI regards JOSEPH.*)

When you stand there...after the clamour and
chaos...amidst the flowing red...the suffocating
smell...what...do you...hear?

JOSEPH: Colours.

HENRI: Colours?

JOSEPH: I hear...colours...

(*HENRI contemplates this for a while.*)

HENRI: Yesterday, after lunch, I took a stroll along the
South wall. I came across a small group of men. They
were having a wanking competition. The first who could
come. Such concentration. Furious intent. I watched,
spellbound. Screwed up faces. Then, just as a young
sergeant started coming, one of the others spotted me
looking at them. The shout went out. Fumbles and
movement. Ant's nest attacked. In the silence, shame.
They, naturally, shamed. But I, even more. I could not
say anything. Nor could they. So, nothing was said, and I
passed on. The next time I saw them, they lay, twisted, in
the pounding sun. Ribbons of flesh. And on their faces:
longing. Such longing. I had spoilt their last pleasure
upon this shattered rock. They died ashamed. **They had
the same faces on.**

JOSEPH: Sire, you despise the men.

HENRI: Yes, fair comment. But I enjoy the drama of it all.
Joseph, what I'm beginning to realise is the correlation
between pain and beauty. It's everywhere. We see an
inspired painting of Jesus on the cross and take it into
battle with us, but for fuck sakes, it's a painting of a man
nailed to a cross!

JOSEPH: Yes, however –

HENRI: The battlefield should not be gaped at in horror.
Rather marvelled for the beauty it possesses – like a
magnificent painting.

JOSEPH: A painting does not leave wives as widows.

HENRI: **It's an idea – why can't you engage with that
you boring bastard!**

(*HENRI seethes whilst JOSEPH remains impassive.
Eventually.*)

You are wounded.

JOSEPH: Yes.

HENRI: Again.

JOSEPH: Yes.

HENRI: Always, again.

JOSEPH: Yes.

HENRI: You must be bored of it by now. All this wounding and healing. I mean, one could accuse you of healing yourself just so that you can wound yourself again. **An obsessive practice!**

(*A silence wherein JOSEPH avoids HENRI's eyes.*)

I know. Sometimes I'm a right fuckwit. I am withdrawing you from active duty for the time being. You are to be a bodyguard.

JOSEPH: Yer wha'?

HENRI: Sometimes your grammar is appalling.

JOSEPH: But, sire –

HENRI: No arguments, Joseph. You've been overexposed lately. Since I can't send you away for a rest, you can do the next best thing and be some rich tart's bodyguard.

JOSEPH: My men –

HENRI: Will be looked after by Rufus. A good man. As you yourself have said. They will be in experienced hands.

JOSEPH: Sire, please –

HENRI: I said no arguments! God, Joseph, you are like a child sometimes –

JOSEPH: **You just wanted me to engage in a debate for Christ sakes!**

HENRI: That's how it is when you're no one – fucking hard.

JOSEPH: I... I...

HENRI: Submit?

(*JOSEPH, after an eternity, nods his head.*)

It's only for a few days and I promise that if it looks like the Turks are going to overrun Christendom, I'll personally call you back.

JOSEPH: Who am I to slave myself to?

(*Voices are heard and SIMON and ANNA enter.*)

HENRI: Just in time! I have just explained to Joseph his new duties.

JOSEPH: Yer gotta be kiddin'?

SIMON: My, his grammar is appalling.

JOSEPH: This cunt?

HENRI: **There are ladies present!**

ANNA: Do not mind me, Sire. Living in a garrison town forces one to listen to all manner of things.

(*JOSEPH sees ANNA for the first time and is shocked visibly. He continues to stare at ANNA throughout.*)

HENRI: You see, already he is mortified at his outburst.

SIMON: I should say so. Language like that in front of a lady! Soldiers are such scum. Are you sure he'll be all right for this job?

HENRI: Bulbous, be quiet. He's worth ten of you.

SIMON: Only with a sword in his hand. What'll he be worth when the fighting's over?

HENRI: Jack shit, I dare say.

SIMON: Well, if that's settled, perhaps we can talk about the plot? In the city?

HENRI: Lascaris can find no evidence.

SIMON: Well, I have evidence.

HENRI: Who?

SIMON: The Jews!

HENRI: It's always the Jews. Are you sure of this…evidence? Or is it a coincidence that they rival you in business?

SIMON: Sire! I would say that there is, it seems, a God after all.

HENRI: (*Laughs.*) Very well. Let's have it.

SIMON: Should we be a bit more private, perhaps?

HENRI: Fine. Joseph, your new mistress. You know your duty.

(*HENRI and SIMON exit. JOSEPH continues to stare at ANNA for some time. Eventually.*)

ANNA: Oh, do stop staring. You look like a hungry cow.

JOSEPH: You are married to him?

ANNA: Ten years.

JOSEPH: That explains a lot about you.

ANNA: You know nothing about me!

JOSEPH: Enough!

ANNA: Admit you have thought about me every day since we met.

JOSEPH: Did you ask for me to be your bodyguard?

ANNA: **Admit it!**

JOSEPH: It is you who chase me –

ANNA: **Admit it!**

JOSEPH: I am a Knight of St John –

ANNA: **Admit it!**

> (*JOSEPH can hardly talk. He pants.*)

Come here.

> (*JOSEPH walks towards ANNA. He moves to touch her.*)

No!

> (*JOSEPH stops, surprised.*)

The past melts away without regret and what seemed so important becomes mundane – who wants yesterday's news? In its place grey limbo and dizziness and euphoria and still you have no idea of what's to come. Save yourself, little man.

JOSEPH: I –

ANNA: Run. For I am merciless and cruel and you will only suffer.

JOSEPH: I –

ANNA: But the things we could achieve, together. Oh, your eyes. Such rare azurian perfection. Joseph, if you were to touch me I would crumble piece by delicate piece, for with you I know that somewhere it is always spring. Our haven amongst the maelstrom. And desire.

JOSEPH: I cannot leave you...

ANNA: No.

JOSEPH: Duty...

ANNA: Yes.

JOSEPH: Duty...

ANNA: Yes.

> (*They stand for a long time staring into one another's eyes.*)

Scene Five

HENRI paces anxiously. TONI and LASCARIS try to reason with HENRI.

TONI: He hasn't eaten nor slept in three days –

LASCARIS: My Lord, take a little food –

TONI: Tried that –

LASCARIS: Perhaps a nap?

TONI: Tried that –

LASCARIS: **I'm gonna do you in a minute –**

HENRI: And the sun became as black as sackcloth
  And the moon became as blood
  And the stars of heaven fell unto the earth –

TONI: I wouldn't mind if he were cracking a few jokes, but this –

LASCARIS: What is it, my Lord?

HENRI: (*Grabbing LASCARIS.*) God blesses the artists –

LASCARIS: What?

HENRI: Sublimity in art –

LASCARIS: I guess so –

HENRI: Mirrors, reflections, prisms –

LASCARIS: What?

HENRI: Encompasses His glory –

LASCARIS: See it now –

HENRI: In paint comes radiance of Divine –

LASCARIS: Wait –

HENRI: A note echoes of unattainable –

LASCARIS: **It's only art –**

HENRI: Representation on earth –

LASCARIS: All right –

HENRI: A canvas His flesh –

LASCARIS: All right –

HENRI: A chapel His body –

LASCARIS: **All right –**

HENRI: Defend the faith by saving art!

TONI: Christ –

LASCARIS: We defend all of it – the people –

HENRI: What know they of art?

LASCARIS: Well –

HENRI: **Their beauty resides in pain!**

LASCARIS: Now, hang on –

HENRI: Unable to create –

LASCARIS: No –

HENRI: Not understanding beauty –

LASCARIS: No –

HENRI: They flourish only –

LASCARIS: **No!**

HENRI: **In the throes of pain!**

TONI: Hardly original –

LASCARIS: These people suffer for you, how –

HENRI: The word of God –

LASCARIS: Espouses kindness –

HENRI: Is not for them –

LASCARIS: Enough!

HENRI: Pain prepares them –

LASCARIS: Enough!

HENRI: To strip away –

LASCARIS: **Enough!**

HENRI: The conceit of their vanities –

LASCARIS: **What about your conceits?**

HENRI: Throw away the surplus food –

TONI: Shit!

HENRI: And the medicines –

TONI: Fuck!

HENRI: Particularly the bandages, Christ's wounds flowed freely –

TONI: Kill the fucker, Lascaris –

HENRI: (*With a dignity not yet seen.*) I am the emissary of the Word, and through me only justice flows. There! (*All three spin around to the direction HENRI suddenly points to.*)
Burning crosses…out of sight…yet…ever present…like…a shadow of cold…

LASCARIS: I just kill…that's all I do…kill…

HENRI: Do it, Lascaris, or I'll rip your heart out with my bare hands and shove it down your rotting mouth till you choke on it.

(*LASCARIS, horrified yet in awe, stumbles out of the room.*)

TONI: A bit strong...that last bit...a bit strong...

HENRI: Everywhere they want me is somewhere else I can't be like a wind I can fill only so many sails and where they are becalmed I feel the most hurt... I am not God...

TONI: Still...

HENRI: I ripped my bible up last night –

TONI: **Destroy a text** –

HENRI: Instead of truth I could only see...

TONI: Destroy a text –

HENRI: When...inside them...deep inside...enveloped...in them...with all the ritual of...and bestial...and...and...

(*TONI notices the change in HENRI.*)

TONI: They grunt like pigs, heaving and twitching –

HENRI: Inside them –

TONI: Writhing contact and skin velvet smooth and wet –

HENRI: Inside them –

TONI: Inside them.

HENRI: What...what's it...like?

(*TONI walks up behind HENRI and whispers something softly into HENRI's ear. TONI abruptly leaves. After a while HENRI begins to howl like a dog, at first softly, then growing ever and ever louder.*)

Scene Six

TONI's house. LUCY is attempting to wash clothes. Children are heard playing. In the distance we also hear the noise of the siege. TONI enters.

TONI: Where are the children?

LUCY: Out back with Leli.

TONI: I'm tired.

LUCY: Did you bring food?

TONI: Does it look like it?

LUCY: You said your job will always provide something – scraps from tables of honour. Your words.

TONI: Lucy, let's not argue. Not now. That mad...man,
Henri, has decreed all surplus food to be thrown away.

LUCY: Jesus Christ.

TONI: And medicine.

LUCY: Mother of God, but the children... Andrea is ill –

TONI: I know.

LUCY: What to do?

TONI: I will get the medicine –

LUCY: How?

TONI: I will get the medicine –

LUCY: If he dies –

TONI: **Enough!**

LUCY: Please, God!

TONI: (*More calmly.*) Lucy, I will get the medicine.

LUCY: In these times?

TONI: Still, there are ways and there are ways.

LUCY: Should... I worry?

TONI: No, not yet. A promise is a promise.

LUCY: I have nothing to give the children.

TONI: I will find something. Let me have a moment's rest.
(*A silence of sorts.*)

LUCY: I am washing clothes in water three weeks old. Soon
there will be more dirt than water.

TONI: Appearances, in the midst of a siege, are not that
important.

LUCY: Not to you, perhaps.
(*A silence of sorts.*)

TONI: Where is Maria?

LUCY: In her room.

TONI: Again?

LUCY: Please, don't start.

TONI: You favour her –

LUCY: – Too much. I know.

TONI: We have other children.

LUCY: Yet you also favour Maria – with your contempt.

TONI: No –

LUCY: Obvious as day –

TONI: She swans around in all that...stuff! Christ! Where does it come from?

LUCY: Not now –

TONI: Not a local boy. Oh, no. How could it be? Could a local boy afford such finery? In these circumstances? I think not.

LUCY: She is a young woman, let her grow. Time enough to be chained –

TONI: What's wrong with a local boy?

LUCY: Nothing. I married one, didn't I?

TONI: But look what's going on! War! Famine! Disease! And she lives like a fairy princess. Perhaps her boyfriends could feed us.

LUCY: Not so loud. She is upset.

TONI: She's upset?

LUCY: Hush. She needs her sleep.

TONI: God in heaven, how did it ever become so?

LUCY: You are tired –

TONI: You'll be surprised what of.

(*A silence of sorts.*)

Why is a local boy not good enough for her? Eh? It is the foreigners who put us in such a position. **Look at us!**

LUCY: And your job –

TONI: Different –

LUCY: How so?

TONI: Different, is all –

LUCY: Again, no answer –

TONI: The Knights help us –

LUCY: Heard it –

TONI: Protect us from the Turks –

LUCY: Heard it –

TONI: When they leave –

LUCY: **Heard it!**

TONI: **– They'll give us our island back!**

LUCY : Still slaving yourself however you look at it.

(*TONI reflects upon this and relents with a sigh.*)

TONI: Is true. I worry about her that's all.

LUCY: I know.

TONI: She is a rose…surrounded by ferociousness.
LUCY: I know.
TONI: I feel so…powerless.
   (*A silence of sorts.*)
LUCY: Why have you stopped kissing me?
TONI: Have I really?
LUCY: Long time.
TONI: I see.
LUCY: And hugs.
TONI: I see.
LUCY: Not everything has to be a grand gesture, you know.
TONI : I see.
LUCY: You fret and worry about the great things and forget
   the important things.
TONI: It seems such an age. When I first saw you. Your
   skin. And your eyes. My, how they shine. I longed so
   much for your touch. Each beat an eternity without you.
   (*LUCY walks over to TONI and sits on his lap.*)
LUCY: And I remember that touch. Your breath on my
   neck. And such words.
TONI: I have lived only for you –
LUCY: Hush –
TONI: I have done terrible things –
LUCY: Hush –
TONI: **Only for you.**
LUCY: I know. Rest a while. Like this.
TONI: I will.
LUCY: Later, you can find some food.
TONI: I will.
LUCY: Speak, gentle words, to Maria.
TONI: I will.
   (*Slowly, as if time itself had stopped, they kiss.*)

Scene Seven

A dark alley. Whispers echo throughout the theatre. Screams. Moans.
Figures dart around the gloom. LASCARIS enters.

LASCARIS: I have arrived.

(*A huge silence. The same as before. LASCARIS is impassive throughout.*)

Repeat. I have –

VOICE: we see

(*Another huge moment in time.*)

LASCARIS: Whilst such silence in the maelstrom could be perceived as God sent, I resent the fact that **I can hear my fucking beard growing!**

VOICE: you assume we waste your time that your time is somehow special unique and that time itself is a commodity valuable beyond thought if only you could hear time and (*Noise again. Somewhere a bell tolls funeral-march in its intonation.*) its shifts and heaves and what you have not acknowledged is folds in time that blur clarity blunt perception and all you do is wait
rose petals rose petals rose petals rose petals

LASCARIS: I was summoned. I have answered that summons.

VOICE: reverberation through time like ripples in a lake some return criss-cross dilemma cascading guilt the future pounding at your heels

LASCARIS: Whilst I accept that such speculation is valid in normal circumstances, at this precise moment bones are smashed, muscles ripped apart, blood spewing, tissue exploding and much more. I cannot impress on you enough that –

VOICE: the air the air Some visions never leave Lascaris a vineyard where screams drip from the air the air the air the leaves like dew with the fog mist wide eyes the pitter-patter of heartbeats and your breath stinking the air the air the air

(*A burst of laughter at once gone.*)

LASCARIS: Orders are –

VOICE: and the chopping and the slicing and the thrusting and the hacking and the slashing with the slime oozing and the stench that never ever goes away

(*A lullaby is heard. LASCARIS slowly lowers his head. The whispering, screams, moans, and even the laughter increase. There is a sense of movement around LASCARIS.*)
snowing rose petals and the air the air the air...

LASCARIS: ...And the innocence...

VOICE: always there is innocence and things unsaid always there are things unsaid you take a step but always there are steps not taken you are a Muslim who now is Christian you are the divide at once the wound at once the healing

LASCARIS: The endless searching and tramping a million miles of solitude –

VOICE: see again the harmonic disunity of life (*A cloud of laugther cut in twain by screams and in the cacophony the sobbing of a child. Abrupt silence.*) slicing slicing annihilation behold the ripples
(*LASCARIS mimes the finding of a dead child and picking her up and holding her close to his chest. He rocks and moans.*)

LASCARIS: **Shame and shame and shame and shame** –

VOICE: the future pounding pounding pounding eternally alone with the void closing in in you have seen the twilight glitter with malice and still you ignore the pain pain pain pain pain pain

LASCARIS: Hammer to a rose stumbling through the waste with the wind of desolation all around **who was ever there?**

VOICE: those who have nothing to say clamour the most what is it you seek as if a puzzle is solvable pounding pounding pounding innocence a little more buried (*Laughter and moans. Movement. LASCARIS slumps to the ground. He begins to crawl.*)

LASCARIS: And I looked into her eyes which reflected the world I wished to live in and hearing my name and knowing oh knowing how it could never be the same again with distance and her eyes and suddenly it dissolved and I stood naked wide eyed how she cut through through me paining blue snowflake tears sitting besides her in the whispering wind her nervous laugh

and eyes how I wished to hold her say things to her and
all the while the wind groaned and paining blue
snowflake tears and silence
(*Silence.*)

VOICE: the stars fell as arrows of flame we walk alone
through the rage and the beauty of it all
the beauty the beauty beauty beauty
amongst you and them pounding pounding pounding
one walks paths of betrayal as you once in time past and
to come betrayed hearts fracture beneath the burden her
you will never see again
eternity spins and spins and spins and spins

LASCARIS: (*Coming to his senses slowly.*) Betrayal? Who?
Who betrays us?

VOICE: everyone at all times betrays to act is to betray not
to act is betrayal empty nights and dreams oh so many
dreams stay outside by retreating inside

LASCARIS: Who? Who?
(*A huge silence. Eventually LASCARIS turns to leave. He
stops and looks back.*)
And the other? The other we talked about? What do I...
I mean...what do...
(*LASCARIS departs to increasing noise and movement.*)

Scene Eight

*SIMON paces the room. He stops to listen, then paces again. Stops,
then paces. ANNA enters.*

SIMON: (*Looking up.*) Oh...

ANNA: Waiting five days seventeen hours if I knew the
time the exact time but time it tumbles never precisely
hardly cheographed no it tumbles and in the reckoning it
moves again like some malevolent thing it tricks so the
minutes don't show **I don't know the minutes** if I did ·
then surely I but it wouldn't matter how could it in such
time how could it matter a minute here or there how
could it matter I mean

(*A period of nothingness descends.*)
I mean

SIMON: Events – heave, groaning under the weight of history – and I – **have you any idea?** You babble – perspective – assume – just assume perspective – a little bit of fucking perspective is all

ANNA: The children miss you.

(*A silence of sorts.*)

SIMON: Hierarchies is what I'm talking about – priorities – (*He suddenly laughs.*) I sent one of the servants – out into the streets – to buy me – to buy me a left-handed hammer – when he returned in failure and distraught – I said 'What I am to do with all these left-handed nails?' – 'Maybe', he said, 'we could use right-handed nails and a right-handed hammer?' – 'In that case,' I said, 'go out and buy some right-handed holes!' – Five fucking hours (*He laughs.*)

ANNA: (*Regarding him. At length.*) You bait him for five hours, before the final humiliating stroke.

SIMON: Humiliating? When he found out he was delighted that I wasn't angry with him – that's all – the officers of the Guard thought it hysterical – they admire my sense of fun in such times – they admire me full stop – **why can't you just smile?**

ANNA: The children miss you.

(*Another interesting silence.*)

SIMON: I don't like it – all this sacrifice – you think it doesn't hurt me? You think I am unscathed by this absence? Anna, the children – **what I wouldn't do –**

ANNA: Then see them.

SIMON: Isn't that your fucking job? I mean, isn't it enough – such times – extremity – Anna, the doors that have opened – I/we elevate – such heights – I will array the stars as baubles in your hair

ANNA: The children.

SIMON: Yes – I will

ANNA: How long is it?

SIMON: You mean you've forgotten? Sorry

ANNA: Another track, then. When you where younger, you were irreverent, childlike.

SIMON: What's changed?

ANNA: Exactly. We have two children already, and like all children they demand to be the centre of the universe, with monstrous egos and mercurial temperaments. Must I look after another? You age –

SIMON: You take life too seriously – relax – what's your problem?

ANNA: If only you could say that about your work. It seems that you want it all your own way – a child marshalling his toys. Pick one up here, drop another off there.

SIMON: But as adult children go, aren't I gorgeous?

ANNA: Your charm wears off. Your mischievous sense of humour wears thin. No matter how you try to succeed you remain still-born.

SIMON: Anna, if it's love – forget it – how could you say I do not love you? After all I have done – (*He goes to hold her. At first she resists, but then relents.*) you are still my white dove, battered and torn by the world – and I, I am the fierce falcon, protecting you – loving you – after all we have shared – memories – the past – these exist in time and space – never to diminish – however much you think we stand apart – we are also locked together – and anyway – how could I leave my poor white dove to fly alone?

(*They kiss.*)

ANNA: Occasionally, I need to be held like this…kissed like this.

SIMON: I know – I will – and the children – tonight – I promise – however hard you think it is right now – it will get better – for we have time on our side

(*ANNA thinks about this for a moment. She smiles and departs. SIMON returns to pacing and listening. Eventually, MARIA enters.*)

MARIA: She does not love you –

SIMON: Christ sakes –

MARIA: She does not love you –

SIMON: Heard you –

MARIA: Mistake sense of duty – the children, maybe – she does not love you –

SIMON: **Heard you –**

MARIA: Maybe she's embarrassed –

SIMON: Eh?

MARIA: Embarrassed about you –

SIMON: Eh?

MARIA: Other men are up to their elbows in blood – gore. But you – well, just look at you –

SIMON: Embarrassed?

MARIA: Maybe she wants a real man –

SIMON: What?

MARIA: Are you a real man, Simon? Or just a little, silly boy?

SIMON: Getting angry –

MARIA: How far can you go, Simon, to get what you want?

SIMON: **Getting angry –**

MARIA: Could you cut flesh –

SIMON: **Angry now –**

MARIA: Watch the blood trickle and flow –

SIMON: **I'm warning you –**

MARIA: (*She produces a knife.*) Cut me.

(*SIMON stares at her, unable to act.*)

Would she do this – for you?

(*MARIA slowly cuts a deep grove in her arm. Blood gushes out. SIMON stares both horrified and transfixed at the sight.*)

This for you –

(*MARIA slowly cuts the other arm, she gasps in pain. SIMON lets out a moan, but is unable to move. He stares at the collecting blood.*)

Come here.

(*SIMON slowly stumbles over to MARIA and stands by her. MARIA smears her blood on SIMON's lips.*)

Taste me.

(*SIMON licks his lips and tastes MARIA's blood.*)

Take it.

(*SIMON takes the knife and stares at it, then at her wounds.*)
Kiss me.
(*SIMON kisses her, then slowly begins to kiss her wounds.
Blood collects around his face. MARIA moans.*)
Cut me.
(*SIMON slowly raises the knife and cuts MARIA across the
breastbone. It isn't a deep cut, more of a scratch. Blood slowly
trickles from it.*)
Deeper.
(*SIMON cuts again, this time deeper. MARIA moans and
SIMON thrusts his head at the new wound licking and kissing
the blood.*)
Fuck me – here, in my own blood…
(*SIMON pushes MARIA to the floor. As he climbs on top of
her, he cuts her across the cheek, and begins to lick and kiss
the blood.*)

Scene Nine

*A small walled garden. We hear the siege, it is quite loud here and
occassionally the theatre rumbles and shakes with the noise of it.
JOSEPH paces clearly agitated. Occassionally he looks up, but there
is no one there. Eventually, ANNA enters, almost silently. JOSEPH
takes a moment before spotting her. During that time she watches
him with a slight smile on her face.*

JOSEPH: At last! Thirty-five minutes late! I was about to
  go.
ANNA: You wouldn't have left.
JOSEPH: With no word I grew worried –
ANNA: That I wouldn't come?
JOSEPH: That you had been taken ill – or worse, hurt,
  maimed perhaps.
ANNA: Would you still care about me if I lost half my
  face?
JOSEPH: Probably more.
ANNA: (*She contemplates this for a moment.*) How tedious!
JOSEPH: If my feelings are –

ANNA: We haven't time for this.

(*A moment.*)

In the formality; in the pretence; **how many times must I avoid your eyes!** And all the while I long just to stand next to you.

(*JOSEPH lowers his head.*)

These moments – fleeting, stolen moments from death – these must not be wasted upon accusations, tantrums, and denial. Nor grand gestures. Here, all between us must be simple, unadorned. Joseph, we itch desire for each other and even the slightest look beat-beat-beats my heart.

JOSEPH: Such longing…seems as if my soul will burst. I see you tremble and I wish to hold you. That is all. Hold you.

ANNA: So much do I need your presence. Without you I am a little lost, incomplete.

JOSEPH: I stood and watched you play with your children yesterday. You did not know I spied so.

ANNA: I felt you near me.

JOSEPH: I am always near you. (*A moment.*) What is to become of us?

ANNA: Joseph –

JOSEPH: I ask for, though nothing is certain, especially now, the hours we part cut and slice me. Walls squeeze in. In the unbearable moments of twilight, I shake and heave. No rest. No rest, for your beauty, upon my mind, plays so.

ANNA: If he knew… Joseph, they burn adulteresses!

JOSEPH: They would have to kill me first.

ANNA: And the children… Sometimes they look at me…and it seems they read my heart and they seem so sad…so sad…

JOSEPH: What could children know of such things?

ANNA: What if someone should see us?

JOSEPH: I am your bodyguard –

ANNA: Sense and logic dictate –

JOSEPH: Listen to the blood in your veins. Know that this and this moment is all time.

ANNA: What about the past?

JOSEPH: Crushed by the intensity of now.

ANNA: With you, I feel safe, secure. It is all so easy. Yet, without you, fears crash around me as the God's thunder.

JOSEPH: I know only this: I have served God and King. The order of St John. Again and again have I been willing to sacrifice my life – for duty. I say this now: you are meaning beyond comprehension, and everything I have done was preparation for loving you.

ANNA: Love?

JOSEPH: Lady, your eyes speak to me and though I am clumsy and foolish, I will love and honour you through any tempest, even death itself. It is not grand gestures – I wish to hold you; kiss you; I wish the children were mine, that you were my wife. Then, you would know love.

ANNA: Kiss me...

(*JOSEPH steps closer to ANNA. They stare into one another's eyes. JOSEPH bends forward to kiss ANNA. Suddenly, a horrendous scream rips through the theatre. JOSEPH and ANNA spring apart. JOSEPH draws his sword. SIMON staggers on. He is covered in blood and spittle hangs from his mouth. He babbles meaningless words and falls to the floor. ANNA rushes over to him.*)

Simon –

JOSEPH: Is he hurt?

AAN: Covered in blood –

JOSEPH: Where is the wound?

ANNA: Simon. Where are you hurt?

(*SIMON babbles.*)

JOSEPH: He's insane –

ANNA: What's happened to him?

JOSEPH: Check for a wound –

ANNA: There is none –

SIMON: Cut my little butterfly cut my little butterfly cut cut cut –

JOSEPH: To a leech quick –

ANNA: There is no wound –

JOSEPH: Then it cannot be his blood –

SIMON: Cut cut cut cut cut –

ANNA: What to do – what to do –

(A huge explosion rocks the theatre. The siege erupts around the scene. We hear siege engines, men screaming and shouting, bugles, drums, and more explosions. SIMON begins shaking and screaming. He cries and babbles. ANNA is frantic. JOSEPH looks around, torn between helping ANNA and rushing off to the fight. LASCARIS enters, sword drawn and blooded. He screams out his orders.)

LASCARIS: Joseph! To the walls! The South wall is breached! To the walls!

JOSEPH: My Lord, Simon Bulbous –

LASCARIS: What matter? Leave this clown! Move, man, move!

(JOSEPH runs off.)

ANNA: Sire, what can I do?

LASCARIS: To a leech. Away with you! This is no time for tears! Go!

(ANNA helps the gibbering SIMON to his feet and takes him off. The noise is becoming louder and closer. LASCARIS looks around as if the fight has spilled into the audience. He screams out his speech.)

No quarter! No quarter! Slaughter the heathen! Maim and hack and slash at their eyes! Rip their throats out! Death to all! Death to all! The sun is red and blood covers the earth! Now is the prophecy fulfilled! Kill! Kill! Kill!

(LASCARIS runs off. Increasing noise. A huge explosion.)

Interval

ACT TWO

Scene One

A dressing station, behind the South wall. Many men lie wounded and dying. The siege is heard distantly. LASCARIS, TONI and JOSEPH accompany HENRI. JOSEPH has a fresh wound. HENRI is trying to 'rally the troops'.

HENRI: I am Alpha and Omega, the beginning and the
end. I will give unto him that is athirst of the fountain of
the water of life freely.
He that overcometh shall inherit all things; and I will be
his God, and he shall be my son.
Well, there's no guarantee. I know that. It's a principle.
You fight for a principle. Not much, I grant you, but
even so...
(HENRI suddenly slumps, as if exhausted.)
History. That's what it's about. History. Even the most
insignificant act... History. History is what we choose it
to be by what we tell of it... I mean...
Your sufferings seem great. Out of proportion to...it
doesn't appear... **Yer fuckin' beat 'em this time, didn't
yer?** Sorry, it's just that...all these decisions and...
Well done. No, I mean it. Well done. The wall was
breached the south wall and you, you heroes repelled the
enemy. Soon we will repair the wall and...
I crave for...no, let me start again. I demand meaning.
That's all. Meaning. Something to satisfy
this...discontent. *(HENRI begins to laugh.)* Sleep, gotta get
some sleep. You think you've got it bad. When do you
think I last ate? Or shat? All you gotta do is stand and
fight. I mean...
Didn't mean that...no, didn't mean that...
It's about beauty, isn't it? Beauty. Look, we are taught
that beauty is the goal. And only the goal is beauty. But
why? Look at the things we ignore, that they say isn't

51

beauty. Did you see the sunrise yesterday? Fucking gorgeous. That's beauty, real beauty. Not some words you can't understand –

LASCARIS: My Lord, perhaps you should –

HENRI: Shhh! You've gotta believe in things you can touch. Not abstraction! Alright, you can't actually touch a sunrise, but…**yer know wha' I mean.**

Beauty is all around. Look at this man. (*HENRI points to a wounded SOLDIER.*) Look at these wounds. Bad, eh? But aren't they beautiful? Why are only some wounds beautiful? I used to know this woman…deformed, ugly as sin…but I…

Pain clears the mind! That's what it's about. Clarity. Here.

(*HENRI kneels next to a dying man. He holds him up and cuddles him as he talks.*)

This man dies. Yes, dies before our eyes. Who is he? Where does he come from? What of his character? Did he enjoy beer? Or women? Was he a pious man? Does it matter? That's the point. His death is all that counts. That is what affects us. These horrendous wounds…see the beauty in them –

LASCARIS: Please, sire –

HENRI: Shut up, Lascaris! These are beautiful wounds because their pain brings him clarity – clarity in the chaos. He sees what we can't see. If only we could see what he sees. Pain focuses the mind. It's that simple. Pain is beauty. Suffering is beauty. Thus, we must suffer pain to enable us to recognise beauty and thus achieve…

Yer gotta understan' why yer fightin'.

No good! Pearls before swine! Fuck it! Fuck you! You want hip-hip-hooray speeches about how marvellous you are. How you are going to beat the heathen. Fucks sake. **Gimme somethin' original.**

These wounds are art! What's the point! Fucking useless!

(*Most of the men are shocked. Some are uncomfortable.
LASCARIS seems deeply upset. TONI files his nails. HENRI
attempts to calm down.*)

You ask, and it is a fair question: what does he know of
these things? Who is he to tell us anything? I say this
unto you. Sometimes, men, special men are needed to
achieve special things. Look around you. We, with about
nine hundred knights and rank and file of no more than
nine thousand, we hold off an army of forty thousand
heathens. They bring war machines; they have plentiful
supplies, fresh water, and medicine. And us? What do we
have? My men, we have me. I alone hold back the forces
of Satan. I alone inspire with feats of heroism. I am at
once everywhere and omnipotent. Believe in me and I
will deliver you. I am your only hope for in me there is
light and I shall repel the darkness.

(*HENRI stands and removes his boots and both of his gloves.*)

I grieve for every death, smile at every kill. I am beside
you at every moment and I know your thought and you
fears and hopes. For I am Alpha and Omega, the
beginning and the end. I will give unto him that is
athirst of the fountain of the water of life freely. He that
overcometh shall inherit all things; and I will be his
God, and he shall be my son.

(*HENRI stands in the with outstretched arms and crossess
his legs in the style of the crucifix. He has the three stigmata.
The SOLDIERS at first amazed, cheer and clap. Some kneel
and make the sign of the cross. Eventually, silence descends.*)

Alright, that's yer lot. Bugger off! Lascaris!

(*LASCARIS and JOSEPH begin to herd the men away. TONI
attends to HENRI. Soon they are alone.*)

Now that was a fucking great speech! Did you see them?

TONI: Saw them.

HENRI: Christ, even Lascaris was impressed and that takes
something, believe me.

TONI: **Saw them.**

HENRI: (*Suddenly holds TONI close to him.*) Do you think I
am a fraud?

TONI: Why would I presume to think anything?

HENRI: Spit in my face.

(*TONI looks into HENRI's eyes for a moment, then spits into his face. HENRI reacts, settles, and signals for TONI to do it again. He does. And again.*)

Scene Two

A small walled garden. ANNA sits alone sewing. The siege is heard distantly. JOSEPH enters.

ANNA: You!

JOSEPH: I hope I am not intruding.

ANNA: I thought you were on duty tonight.

JOSEPH: It was quiet. I managed to slip out.

ANN: My, how things change.

JOSEPH: Would you like me to go? I could always –

ANNA: No! Stay. Now that you are here. He could come at any time.

JOSEPH: I am your bodyguard.

ANNA: You may get into trouble if caught.

JOSEPH: There are few people who could do that.

ANNA: Are you trying to impress me?

JOSEPH: What would be the point? Leave him.

ANNA: Don't be ridiculous!

JOSEPH: You don't love him –

ANNA: I never said that.

JOSEPH: Well, do you?

ANNA: Not love, but –

JOSEPH: But what? Either you do or don't.

ANNA: Roots run deep.

JOSEPH: Oh, come on! We live this life once, you would slave yourself for eternity out of...what? Duty?

ANNA: What about the afterlife?

JOSEPH: I don't want to discuss theology just now.

ANNA: Aren't you a Knight of God?

JOSEPH: Why are you doing this?

ANNA: Logic –

JOSEPH: God's sake –

ANNA: Swearing now! I am teaching you bad habits.

JOSEPH: Don't mock me! Nothing gives you the right to
mock me.

(*A moment.*)

Sorry.

ANNA: Don't be. I almost liked that Joseph.

JOSEPH: If we are to be together –

ANNA: It is not as simple as that!

JOSEPH: You love me, yes?

ANNA: Done this.

JOSEPH: Answer the question!

ANNA: **Done this!**

JOSEPH: You do! You said you do. And if that is true, you
must want to be with me.

ANNA: Joseph, think sensibly, just for a moment. I am
married to the richest merchant in Malta. He has
influence. Your Henri being one of his friends –

JOSEPH: Never!

ANNA: And we are at war. We can't even leave this island.
Surrounded by enemies. I have two children. What do
you expect me to do?

JOSEPH: (*Sighs.*) I don't know.

ANNA: Sometimes, no matter how we feel, there is a
process to go through. I understand your frustration, but
until some things change, nothing else can.

JOSEPH: If he died –

ANNA: (*Laughing.*) You are to become a murderer as well?

JOSEPH: Why not? It's what I do best.

(*A silence. The guns are heard distantly.*)

ANNA: With you I know I could be happy. Happier than I
have ever been. Perhaps it will be destined to happen. We
shall see. In the meantime, we wait…and enjoy the
moments we have together.

JOSEPH: I long so much to be near you.

ANNA: I know. It is the same for me.

JOSEPH: I dreamt of you. It was snowing. Strange animals
prowled around us. But I held you tight to me. And you

cried and crystal tears fell upon my shoulders. And the
wind howled through the trees and your eyes sang to me,
touching this and then that part of my heart. When I
awoke, it seemed as if desolation had settled upon me,
for in the waking I had lost you.

ANNA: I am here now for you.

JOSEPH: If I were to die –

ANNA: Hush.

JOSEPH: At the walls –

ANNA: Hush.

JOSEPH: Crushed by artillery –

ANNA: **Hush.**

JOSEPH: I would be happy to face oblivion, for you.

ANNA: Your words ensnare me and I cherish each one.
Joseph, we shall be happy.
(*An explosion is heard distantly.*)

JOSEPH: I must go. It seems the Turks have awoken.

ANNA: Don't go.

JOSEPH: I must –

ANNA: I lied. He is not coming back tonight. I am alone.
Stay with me.

JOSEPH: I can't –

ANNA: Well, love melts so quickly –

JOSEPH: Anna, I can't –

ANNA: Go and play soldiers –

JOSEPH: Please, Anna –

ANNA: You come here and profess…such things. Yet in
your heart…what really lies in your heart, Joseph?

JOSEPH: I love you. You know that. Please don't do this –

ANNA: Why not? You wish me to give up everything for
you, well what about you? What will you give up for
me?

JOSEPH: I don't understand. You know I have to go. This
is no game –

ANNA: Then what is it?

JOSEPH: So be it! I will stay!

ANNA: (*Surprised, despite herself.*) Really? You will stay?

JOSEPH: If it proves to you about how I feel, then yes.

ANNA: Sit next to me.

(*JOSEPH sits next to ANNA. Guns are heard. Another explosion.*)

My maid dropped my lace dress in some mud today. It is ruined. With no fresh water, how could she get the stains out?

JOSEPH: Hmm.

ANNA: One cannot get carrots for love or money.

JOSEPH: Shocking.

ANNA: Oh, that reminds me, my youngest drew a delightful picture. It showed the sun in the sky, and the waves crashing onto the beach. Quite an artist.

JOSEPH: I must see it someday.

ANNA: (*Bursting out with laughter.*) Oh, Joseph, you are so lovely!

JOSEPH: What?

ANNA: Did you really think I would stop you from going?

JOSEPH: But I thought –

ANNA: You must love me ever so much.

JOSEPH: You know I do.

ANNA: Go, and come back later. We shall eat together.

JOSEPH: (*Smiling.*) I shall bring fresh bread –

ANNA: And…take care…

(*JOSEPH departs. ANNA returns to her sowing, humming to herself.*)

Scene Three

SIMON sits alone. Some of the clothes he wears are female items. He is obviously drunk or drugged. His arms show many cuts and some of the cuts still bleed. Others have been bandaged poorly. Some of the bandages are filthy. Indeed, SIMON looks generally dirty and wears a debauched look. He laughs inanely. Spittle dribbles from his mouth. He is attempting to fill a pipe, but making a complete mess of it. He laughs. The three TURKS enter. They stand and watch him for a moment, disdain upon their faces.

TURK 3: You should have let me kill him a long time ago.

TURK 2: Then we wouldn't have the information –

TURK 3: There are always others – these Christians, sell anybody for nothing.

TURK 1: Wasn't it pieces of silver?

TURK 3: Scum like this wants power. Look at him. To think he believes that we are his friends.

TURK 1: No. Not even he is that stupid. Beware him. That is what I have been told.

(*TURK 3 snorts in derision. SIMON hears this and sees the TURKS.*)

SIMON: Ah, gentlemen. Do you smoke? It's just that I can't seem to get the stuff in. I think this fucking thing ain't got a hole that works – bit like my wife.

TURK 1: Everything is ready. Your ship and a crew await. Gold, to the amount you requested, is stored upon it. You will have papers guaranteeing you safe passage. Everything is ready.

SIMON: Wanted to be an artist once. Painting. Quite good I thought. Even studied under a master for a while. But you see art doesn't change anything. Does it? Don't stop wars, or famine. Can't cure the ill. Fuck me, it can't even get you laid! They say art is powerful, but they are wrong. It is those who control art that have the power. That's what its about – control. And control comes to those who can afford it. I want to be able to control art, because, in a way, it's artistic. Get it?

(*SIMON laughs. The TURKS glare at him.*)

TURK 1: Give us the information about the defences on the East wall.

(*SIMON continues to laugh.*)

Now!

SIMON: Did you enjoy the titbit I gave you last time you were here?

TURK 1: Look –

SIMON: Wanna see her again? I'm sure she'd love to see you lot again. Maria!

TURK 2: (*Advances threateningly.*) Give me the information or I'll –

SIMON: What! What will you do – fucker! Think you can hurt me! Me! Do you know who listens to me! Your fucking Sultan, that's who! So don't threaten me you little shit or I'll have you balls sliced off and served up for tomorrow's lunch. Got it, cunt?

(*The TURKS admit defeat gracelessly. MARIA enters. She has many bandages. Blood stains appear on the fresh cuts. She walks as if unsteady. Clearly she is in a lot of pain.*)

Darling. How nice of you to join us.

TURK 2: God in Heaven! Was she attacked?

SIMON: Only by Cupid. Or should I say Venus.

(*SIMON casually cuts MARIA, who squirms slightly but does not cry out. The TURKS flinch at the cut. They stare with open hostility toward SIMON.*)

Well, perhaps we won't repeat our little game today. I'm afraid that anything too vigorous might split her open!

(*SIMON laughs to himself. The TURKS stand not knowing what to do anymore.*)

Anyway, enough of this tart. Fill this for me.

(*SIMON gives MARIA the pipe. SIMON pulls out some papers. They have blood stains on them.*)

Sorry, about the…well, anyway. It's all there. Tell your boss that an hour before the attack I shall leave the city and meet the guard party. I will expect to be on my ship before the attack begins. Is that clear? Good, now fuck off.

(*The TURKS bow and depart. TURK 3 glares at SIMON as he leaves.*)

Have you finished that yet?

MARIA: It is ready. Shall I light it?

SIMON: Yes, I need something to soothe my head. I am so exhausted! The work that I do – no one appreciates it!

MARIA: (*Gives SIMON the lit pipe.*) Hush now. Work is over for the day. Night approaches and we shall play.

SIMON: Yes, I need to relax.

MARIA: When you are ready, I shall bathe your wounds and change the bandages.

SIMON: Naughty-naughty. I know what you want.

MARIA: I want only what you want.

SIMON: Then you must cut me...on my arse! I want you to play with me, tease the point up me – cut me a little.

MARIA: If I cut you there it may never heal.

SIMON: Then every day you'll have to apply some balm with your finger...or maybe two...

(*They laugh. SIMON smokes.*)

MARIA: When do they attack?

SIMON: Silly girl. Leave the business to me.

MARIA: I am just worried about my family.

SIMON: Family?

MARIA: Should I tell them to pack anything?

SIMON: Maria, they are not coming.

MARIA: But you said –

SIMON: Never mind that. Time changes things. There is to be no family.

(*A silence.*)

MARIA: You are not taking me, are you?

SIMON: Must we talk, I am so tired –

MARIA: Answer.

SIMON: If only you knew how hard I work –

MARIA: **Answer!**

SIMON: My darling, if only I could follow you to where you must go. Sweet dreams.

(*SIMON kisses MARIA and as he does so he produces a knife and stabs her in the lower stomach. He continues to kiss her as she dies despite her struggles. Eventually she goes limp and dies. SIMON lets her fall to the ground. He howls.*)

Scene Four

TONI's house. Evening. LUCY clears a table. In the distant we hear the noise of the siege. TONI enters.

TONI: Is she back yet?

LUCY: No.

TONI: I don't know who else to try. What did the note say again?

LUCY: That a friend had been hurt and that she would be
    looking after her for a while.

TONI: **Her?**

LUCY: That's what it said.

TONI: But I've been to all of her friends. Not one of them
    has seen Maria.

LUCY: Toni, I'm shaking so inside. Perhaps…

TONI: We know where she is, only we don't know – if you
    see what I mean.

LUCY: You still think –

TONI: Yes! Of course! She's with him! Fancy boy!

LUCY: If only we knew who he was –

TONI: This is what happens when we allow children to run
    wild. You should keep more control over them. I didn't
    mean that…you know…

LUCY: Perhaps you could ask…maybe –

TONI: It's obviously a foreigner. Obviously. I will. I will go
    and ask Vallette if he has heard anything… God! The
    embarrassment!

LUCY: Toni, if she has stayed with him all this time, then
    she might have also…what if she is of child?

TONI: If the bastard doesn't marry her I'll get Vallette to
    string him up by his balls.

LUCY: You look tired. Sit awhile. I will fetch you
    something to eat.

TONI: I'm not hungry. (*TONI sits down at the table.*) Perhaps
    some wine?

LUCY: Here, it's the last of it.

TONI: I will get some more.

LUCY: It is good that you serve Vallette. We eat better than
    anyone around here. Meat, on a daily basis! Imagine it,
    some haven't eaten meat in weeks.

TONI: Let us not dwell upon it.

LUCY: If only there were fresh vegetables. The children
    need fresh vegetables.

TONI: Are the children sick?

LUCY: No. Asleep. (*TONI drinks. Cannon are heard.*) Toni, I
    dreamt –

TONI: Not again! Please!

LUCY: Just listen –

TONI: Lucy. Your dreams mean nothing. **Guns have no time for premonitions!**

LUCY: Something isn't right –

TONI: It's called war –

LUCY: In this house! I sense death in this house!

TONI: No one has died –

LUCY: Yet!

TONI: Lucy, Maria's vanishing act has upset you –

LUCY: **I smell it!**

TONI: – we are all anxious, but we must keep control –

LUCY: I am never wrong –

TONI: If others hear this they will say witchcraft! You know that! Vallette and his mob look for any reason to string people up. **Sets an example!** Lucy, I don't want to see your rotting corpse at the end of a rope. Stay with me, and be quiet.

(*LUCY rises. She begins to exit, then stops and turns toward TONI.*)

LUCY: I know what I know.

(*She exits. TONI sighs, finishes his drink and stands. TONI crosses to a large dresser and begins to move it away from the wall. A curtain is revealed behind it. When TONI is satisfied that he is alone, he opens the curtain. A near-naked man is seen. His arms are tied by chains to the ceiling and he hangs limp. His body is covered with horrific scars and cuts. Some makeshift bandages are hanging from him. He is gagged and his legs are tied together. The man is unconscious. TONI slaps him a couple of times and the man awakes and moans. He recognises TONI and begins to scream and jerk about. The man's screams are muffled by the gag. TONI regards him for a moment or two.*)

TONI: We've been through this before. Remember? Any noise, any attempt at noise – I kill you. There is no escape. You know this. We've been through this before.

(*The man becomes still and silent. He regards TONI with hostility.*)

Better. The gag is coming off – I need to talk. Yes?
(*The man nods. TONI removes the gag. Silence.*)
You heard the conversation? Of course you didn't. Silly
question. Pointless. However, in these times, even
pointless questions have their place. My daughter is
missing. I believe she is shacked up with one of your
Knights. Do you know who it is?

MAN: No. I don't even know your daughter.

TONI: Why should I believe you?

MAN: Why should I lie? Look at me!

TONI: Fair comment.

MAN: Why are you doing this?

TONI: Heard this.

MAN: Just let me go –

TONI: Heard this!

MAN: I won't tell anyone –

TONI: **Heard this!** You think I owe you an explanation?
Look who's tied up here.

MAN: **You feed your family my flesh!**

TONI: You will never believe how succulent you are –
better than the rest –

MAN: My God! How many others?

TONI: Who cares.

MAN: You work in a privileged position – you could get all
the food you want –

TONI: You think I'm good enough to get that particular
perk? I'm a local. Scum. Vallette doesn't care about me. I
serve. Am replaceable.

MAN: But even so –

TONI: You parasites feed off us – well I am returning the
compliment.

MAN: We are here to help you –

TONI: By starving us! By enslaving us! I would hate to have
you as an enemy if this is friendship.

MAN: They will notice that I am missing.

TONI: (*Laughing.*) It's a siege! How would they know that
you were here? They'll assume you're dead – like the
others.

MAN: By God's grace I implore you –

TONI: Don't bring that bastard into it. Time enough for him.

MAN: You break His laws –

TONI: And what are you doing? Slaughtering Turks in every conceivable way.

MAN: You can't compare the war to this!

TONI: Sliding scales of morality – who is to judge?

MAN: You're mad!

TONI: Actually, I'm the sanest among us.

(*TONI replaces the gag. The MAN begins to scream and thrash about. His screams are muffled and his movement restricted. TONI pulls out a stool, upon which is a bowl. He produces a long knife and moves behind the MAN. TONI begins to slice flesh off the MAN's back. The MAN thrashes around violently. TONI drops the flesh into the bowl and continues. The MAN eventually passes out.*)

Scene Five

A graveyard. HENRI sits by a freshly dug grave. He regards the grave for some time. The siege is heard distantly. ANNA enters and is surprised to see HENRI there.

ANNA: If I disturb –

HENRI: No. Not at all. I always have time for…well, you know…

(*They sit. Eventually.*)

This is Steiner. In the grave. Friend of mine – no, not a friend. A sort of…well, you know…

ANNA: So many dead…

HENRI: Some Turk hacked his head in two – spilling his brains all over the place. Which is strange, because that was the one thing I was sure that Steiner didn't have.

ANNA: They all say that you are a saint.

HENRI: Really?

ANNA: Yes, they revere you.

HENRI: They threw me in jail once. My temper, they said. I must learn to control my temper.

ANNA: Have you?

HENRI: Threw me in jail, starved me, tortured me for a while, and then, ten years later, made me commander of the Eastern army. What a career.

ANNA: Fate...

HENRI: Money, actually.

ANNA: Who you know –

HENRI: What you know would be better. Education, that's the thing. I was promoted because I studied my enemies, and in battle anticipated their every move. I got so good that they had to promote me – I suppose the loot I gave them helped.

ANNA: Should I educate my sons?

HENRI: Put it this way: the more they know, the less they can be deceived. Of course, they won't be able to do anything about it, but at least they'll know they are lied to. They repress knowledge, you know.

ANNA: They?

HENRI: The things they hide from people. As if the world could get worse than it is now by knowing the truth.

ANNA: But what if everything you ever believed in was wrong – what then?

HENRI: Most people change their beliefs like shirts. Fashion, you know. Stability is not necessarily a bad thing.

ANNA: You're a dangerous man to lead us.

HENRI: Us? I wonder if it'll be us if we lost.

ANNA: Losing would be a setback for civilisation.

HENRI: Whose civilisation? There are many – those that have been and those yet to come. We are transitory. That's all. We own nothing. We are masters of nothing. Only responsibility is ours.

ANNA: Responsibility?

HENRI: Call it duty if you will.

ANNA: To whom?

HENRI: Everybody and everything. We act like petulant children, going mad whilst the adults are away. Which generation will it be that accepts the burden of responsibility?

ANNA: We need more men like you.

HENRI: Bollocks! Half the time I'm scared and the other half out of ideas. Of course, I shall deny I ever said that.

ANNA: Naturally.

HENRI: I doubt the Bible. Does that shock you? It ought to for it shocked me when I realised. The damn thing's so...fragmented. How can I extol men to die for it when it plainly doesn't make sense?

ANNA: It is metaphorical, surely?

HENRI: Many years ago, my father used to make me sweep up the leaves that fell into our garden. Now, our garden was huge, and it used to take me hours to complete the job. I even started getting up early in the morning so I could finish at a reasonable time. Day in day out I swept. Autumn was the worst. Imagine it. Why do I have to do this, father? I asked. To strengthen your moral fibre, a major part of becoming a man. And also because it makes the garden look untidy. I thought about this and came up with a solution. When my father went away for a couple of days I chopped down all the trees. I cut them up and sold off the wood for a healthy profit. I had acted like an adult: I made a rational decision based upon the evidence before me and acquired a business head. I also made the garden look tidy forever. When my father returned, I showed him my work. He was furious, so much so that he enlisted me in the Knights there and then. He even used the money I made to buy me a commission. I never saw him again.

ANNA: What does that have to do with the bible?

HENRI: I haven't the slightest, but it's a good story.

ANNA: I hate my children.

HENRI: Most do. Children represent the lost dreams of parents.

ANNA: I hate them for their youth.

HENRI: Yes, it's inexcusable that they should have it and we don't.

ANNA: You're a liar, aren't you?

HENRI: The worst – I sometimes believe the lies.

ANNA: What holds you together?

HENRI: Fear.

ANNA: A lie.

HENRI: You?

ANNA: I am a woman.

HENRI: You must understand that everything I have said has its opposite and that that opposite isn't necessarily wrong or incorrect. Indeed, the mere fact that there are countless variations and fragments of truth makes... I mean...well, you know...

ANNA: You think it's all important, all this...stuff. It isn't. You know that, don't you?

HENRI: I am beginning to suspect it.

ANNA: We know what is important. It's a matter of admitting it. That's all.

HENRI: And if it's wrong?

ANNA: It won't be.

HENRI: I see...such things –

ANNA: So what? I do incredible things every day.

HENRI: But I am history and you –

ANNA: Yes? What am I?

HENRI: Disconcerting.

ANNA: For all your posturing, you have nothing.

HENRI: I am scared.

ANNA: So am I.

HENRI: What to do?

ANNA: (*Gets up.*) When I look at the stars, alone, at night, my soul shivers so that I feel I will fall apart – piece by trembling piece. But I don't. Instead, I fall asleep.
(*ANNA exits. HENRI contemplates awhile then laughs loudly.*)

Scene Six

JOSEPH paces anxiously. He is muttering to himself. Every now and then he looks up yet seems disappointed that no one is there. The siege is heard quite close and it is louder than before – as if an attack is in progress nearby. Eventually, a wounded soldier – BERNARD – enters.

BERNARD: Sire! Sire! I have found you at last!

JOSEPH: What? Oh, Bernard. What is it?

BERNARD: The Eastern wall buckles under the assault of the heathen. Thousands scream out of the dark –

JOSEPH: God sakes, you shit yourselves over noises?

BERNARD: They attack –

JOSEPH: Do you hold?

BERNARD: Yes, Sire, but –

JOSEPH: Then go back and lend a hand – or does your message hide fear, Bernard?

BERNARD: I was sent, Sire. My Lord Kern sent me here. He fears the attack is too much for his art. He defers to you, Sire. Commanding officer in charge.

JOSEPH: Kern has handled many such sorties –

BERNARD: More than that!

JOSEPH: And furthermore is trained to defend against ruses –

BERNARD: **More than that!**

JOSEPH: Are you deliberately fucking me off? (*JOSEPH notices something offstage.*) Now go! Go!
(*BERNARD reluctantly leaves but does so with bad grace. ANNA enters almost immediately. JOSEPH rushes over to her.*)
Four hours yesterday! Another three today! And still you didn't come!

ANNA: You are following me now; haranguing me outside of my door –

JOSEPH: What other way is there to see you? Four days –

ANNA: You are supposed to be on duty –

JOSEPH: I decide that! (*A silence of inconsequence.*) A silly thing to say. Yes, I should be at the Eastern wall.

ANNA: Then go –

JOSEPH: I am told that I am no longer your bodyguard.
   (*A few moments elapse wherein the noise of the siege is heard.*)
   Well?

ANNA: Not my doing. I was told –

JOSEPH: Well?

ANNA: – that all men were needed –

JOSEPH: **Well?**

ANNA: It's embarrassing. Us. Embarrassing.

JOSEPH: Are you shocked? You said it would be.

ANNA: Joseph, people –

JOSEPH: Fuck 'em!

ANNA: (*Laughs.*) My, how you have changed!

JOSEPH: (*Suddenly.*) In the waiting cascade upon cascade
   wave upon wave the dark is so huge and dazed and
   splintered stumbling in a lost place the black and voices
   echoes of echoes visions in my mind of touches and
   caresses where are you now as if the stars tumbled from
   the skies and the pitter-patter of hurt raining down
   broken as rainbow light never to be put together again
   shaking and trembling to hear your voice your eyes
   watched eternally for your glimpse and only shadows
   and fears missed you again the slightest glance a word
   flow my tears for in the grey and absence silence calls
   malicious and cutting to be with you to be something
   time itself is staggered in your presence flowers bow
   before you the sun humbled sing to me your colours and
   shades bathe me in your twilight hues for if you are the
   song then I am the rhythm

ANNA: Words of wonder and like lace butterflies they will
   perish before the cruel sun. Go and play soldiers.
   (*JOSEPH is crushed. LASCARIS enters, livid.*)

LASCARIS: What the fuck are you doing here?

JOSEPH: I...

LASCARIS: Are you wounded, man?

JOSEPH: I...

LASCARIS: A hundred of your men lost! Where the fuck
   were you?

JOSEPH: A hundred?

LASCARIS: Many more wounded! A full scale attack!
Thousands of the screaming bastards! Where were you?

JOSEPH: I...

LASCARIS: Desertion is punishable by death!

JOSEPH: No, I...

LASCARIS: So is fucking around with some other guy's
wife.

JOSEPH: (*Bows his head in shame.*) I know...

LASCARIS: Get to the wall. We'll talk later.

(*JOSEPH turns to exit but stops and looks at ANNA.*)

JOSEPH: Why?

LASCARIS: **Go!**

(*JOSEPH exits. After a moment LASCARIS turns to ANNA.
He regards her for a while.*)

You're a fucking bitch.

ANNA: Is that all you can –

LASCARIS: **Fuckin' bitch!**

ANNA: What is it that you fear about me. Lascaris?

LASCARIS: Fear?

ANNA: Yes. It's obvious. The looks. The glares. Short
words. Silences. You may think you hate me, but it is
fear all the same.

LASCARIS: The audacity of spite.

ANNA: Tell me –

LASCARIS: Won't waste my time –

ANNA: We are the same – you and I. Not opposites. The
same.

LASCARIS: In the foaming madness one can excuse...but
this?

ANNA: I see your loneliness. The indecision of
humiliation.

LASCARIS: Bollocks.

ANNA: We both view the other. We stand both inside and
outside. The same.

LASCARIS: (*Falters.*) When I was lost, they...punished
me –

ANNA: I know.

LASCARIS: And solace seemed so distant. As in a dream, tumbling.

ANNA: I know.

LASCARIS: We must fear love.

ANNA: Why?

LASCARIS: And compassion. Especially that.

ANNA: Being hated – I cannot stand that.

LASCARIS: Joseph?

ANNA: As much a fraud as I am.

LASCARIS: They say a relief force approaches. When it comes, these games shall cease.

ANNA: Which games?

(*The sound of the siege grows louder.*)

Scene Seven

SIMON sits alone on the floor. He appears to be playing with a child's doll. He strokes its long hair and talks nonsense to it. SIMON wears almost excusively women's clothes and we recognise many of MARIA's items on him. He is dirty and looks as if he hasn't slept for a while. The siege is heard.

SIMON: Good girl good girl (*Laughs.*) buzz-buzz-buzzy-buzz-buztt were are your sheep little one-one-bun-bum (*Laughs.*) now if it rained wash away wash away all the little boys nasty boys cock-cock-cock bitch with horrid stains upon your dress little peek-peeky (*SIMON looks up the doll's dress and laughs.*) no so many questions and things little girls can't understand-stan-stan-the-little-man oh I don't want to eat just now gotta play-play-may-may may I marry you silly little girl marry who me I'm honoured (*Laughs.*) if only it rained wash the cuts clean-mean-bean (*SIMON howls like a dog.*) cut you so much so much pretty face mince-mince and run the red gravy run-run-run and I miss you so much so much (*Laughs.*) right-handed holes right-handed holes was your hole right-handed me dear?

(*SIMON laughs and howls. He seems both distraught and happy. ANNA enters with JOSEPH. When JOSEPH sees SIMON, JOSEPH is incredulous.*)

JOSEPH: All the saints in heaven.

ANNA: I lie not. You see how it is.

JOSEPH: What has happened to this fool?

ANNA: Mind not his physical state – there is worse than this to come.

JOSEPH: Worse? How? He gibbers like an imbecile.

ANNA: Games of exquisite and precise risk tumble and fall.

SIMON: Blow away rain blow away rain slash her face red and feel the pain –

ANNA: He has been like this since I found him.

JOSEPH: What am I to do?

SIMON: I didn't mean it no no not mean it really (*SIMON picks up the doll and strokes its hair.*) the eyes you see yes eyes how they lie can't resist the lies only thing you can depend on

ANNA: Save him.

JOSEPH: What?

ANNA: Save him...for me.

SIMON: Buzzity-buzzity-buzz-buzz-buzz so pretty and snow falling who said love was enough and a goblin on my shoulder (*Laughs.*) if the sun refused to shine...it'd be dark (*Laughs.*)

ANNA: Joseph, you have always known it would be like this. You decide. You know what you have to do...now is the time.

JOSEPH: But...

ANNA: He plays on both sides and Turks call him friend. He has betrayed everyone.

JOSEPH: Then my duty –

ANNA: Is to me.

(*Silence. SIMON dribbles and plays with the doll. JOSEPH stares at ANNA.*)

JOSEPH: I...do not know...what to say...

ANNA: Love me –

JOSEPH: I do –

ANNA: Then save him.

JOSEPH: (*Slowly, as if in a dream.*) Yes... I will...

(*SIMON howls and begins to both laugh and cry.*)

SIMON: Flow flow the red flow flow the red for me

ANNA: Come, my husband. Let us depart.

(*With great effort ANNA manages to lift SIMON and begins to help him offstage. JOSEPH watches transfixed. As ANNA and SIMON pass JOSEPH, SIMON leans over to JOSEPH and begins to stroke JOSEPH's hair.*)

SIMON: **Loser!**

(*ANNA and SIMON exit. JOSEPH is unable to move but continues to stare after them. After a suitable time, LASCARIS enters.*)

LASCARIS: Joseph.

JOSPEH: Yes...

LASCARIS: Do you have business here?

JOSEPH: I... I...

LASCARIS: In confidence I tell you, I am here to arrest the traitor. News has reached me. He is to be found here. You may help. I hope it gets violent.

JOSEPH: I... I... I am he...

(*LASCARIS glares at JOSEPH.*)

LASCARIS: No time for foolishness –

JOSEPH: I am he...

(*LASCARIS digests this. He slowly draws out his sword.*)

LASCARIS: Unbuckle your sword.

(*JOSEPH remains unable to move.*)

Now!

(*As if awakening from a dream JOSEPH unbuckles his sword.*)

It is evident that you lie, but also evident that you know something. Tell me.

JOSEPH: I am he –

LASCARIS: Tell me!

JOSEPH: I am he –

LASCARIS: I command it!

JOSEPH: I am he...

(*LASCARIS slowly shakes his head.*)

LASCARIS: What spell has she? Very well, I strip you of your commission. **Tell me for fuck sakes!**

JOSEPH: I am he –

LASCARIS: Why protect him? Of all the perverted... I know...just one word...**let me hear one word**... Joseph, I mean to take your status away. Complete humiliation. Think of your family. **Christ, you prick, think about this!**

(*JOSEPH lowers his head.*)

This traitor...gave information...to the Turks...a secret entrance into the city...surprise attack...only we got there first...even so...many men killed...carnage and fury...boiling blood...they will hang you if you admit to this...

JOSEPH: I hear... I hear a counter-attack is to be launched from the Western wall.

LASCARIS: It is possible.

JOSEPH: I wish to go –

LASCARIS: It is suicide! A feint to draw attention away from the weakness in the North wall –

JOSEPH: **I wish to go.**

(*A moment of thought.*)

LASCARIS: Yes...go.

(*LASCARIS exits.*
Falling to his knees, JOSEPH tries to pray but cannot. After a struggle he suddenly cries out.)

JOSEPH: Anna!

(*A gust of laughter drifts overhead.*)

Scene Eight

ANNA sits listening to the distant siege. She plays with a bracelet. Time heaves. JOSEPH enters. He looks exhausted and wears different, plainer, clothes.

JOSEPH: I am sorry that I am late.

ANNA: These things...you know.

(*They listen for a while.*)

JOSEPH: I saw a flower. A blue flower.

ANNA: Where?

JOSEPH: The South wall is badly breached. A huge hole.
We pack it with men. Bricks of flesh. Fluids run deep
there. In the midst –

ANNA: I see.

JOSEPH: I miss you. As if time stands still –

ANNA: Enough.

JOSEPH: Wait, let me explain –

ANNA: **Enough!**

(*The siege is heard.*)

JOSEPH: Strange tales distort his standing.

ANNA: Little matter.

JOSEPH: You...nurse him?

ANNA: I try. He has a tendency to vanish at odd moments.
As if he were never there in the first place. I search often
for his howls and grunts. Among the dead...among the
dead...

JOSEPH: Dedication has its own rewards –

ANNA: I loved the way you protected me – held me.
Knowing you were there...it made me glow.

JOSEPH: I failed you –

ANNA: Listen. We were always to be dazzled, twisted
among such eddies. We produced possibilities.

JOSEPH: But you remain nursing him –

ANNA: It was always to be such... I warned you.

(*An explosion stops them from talking. Then.*)

JOSEPH: I have volunteered.

ANNA: Look, the sun dies –

JOSEPH: Certain death –

ANNA: Agonising reds –

JOSEPH: **How can you stomach it?**

ANNA: You always wanted it! Now you have it! Jagged
selfishness!

JOSEPH: But our love –

ANNA: Speak not of it. Some things we bury because it is
valuable.

JOSEPH: I see.

(*The siege is heard.*)
I shall not see you again.
(*The siege is heard.*)
The men are angry with me. Angry for failing. I have no
one now.
ANNA: We always end up alone. No matter how we pack
our lives, we end alone. It is as if death needs no
audience.
JOSEPH: I am scared…to die alone…
ANNA: Look not to me for comfort. That is beyond me…
(*Another huge explosion nearby. JOSEPH and ANNA watch.*)
JOSEPH: If I had a token, a memento, perhaps your
bracelet –
ANNA: For what?
JOSEPH: Courage?
ANNA: Oh dear.
JOSEPH: Please.
ANNA: No.
JOSEPH: Please!
ANNA: **No!**
JOSEPH: You deny me this, at the last, you deny me this.
ANNA: But think how much I gave.
(*JOSEPH lowers his head, as if in pain. The siege is heard.*)
When I was a child such times innocence and fear
through the blurring it always snowed and the scented
fires still haunt my dreams oh the soldiers came and
went they always do and though they burned with red
spite still it snowed and in the midst of silent white roses
grew and they were my roses such lethal fragility
bloodstains upon the silk and my despair was a fainting
lady for as she and her lord rode through my town her
fit was such that a bed was called for and my parents of
equal rank put up the lady and her lord was mighty
afraid and the doctor prescribed a healing brew and rose
petals made up the large part and my parents went and
decimated my roses for the whims of a pale dreamer and
upon hearing this I burned the bushes with green rage
and collected the ashes and freed the ashes upon the west

wind and it was as if the roses had never existed except those in my mind

JOSEPH: I see.

(*JOSEPH turns to leave but as he does so ANNA rushes to him and turns him around to face her. She stares at him intently and then suddenly kisses him passionately.*)

ANNA: You are all I ever wanted and by dying, I die also.

JOSEPH: I...

(*JOSEPH, flushed with pride, slowly turns and exits. The siege is heard.*)

Scene Nine

(*HENRI and TONI walk on. HENRI stumbles and TONI catches him. HENRI tries to talk but spits in TONI's face instead. TONI slaps HENRI. HENRI laughs. TONI slaps him again, harder. HENRI sobs. He holds on to TONI. Eventually, HENRI stops crying. The siege is heard.*)

HENRI: Needed. Admit that. Needed. Lancing a boil. Still, rather hard, in the circumstances...needed.

TONI: The men will be here soon.

HENRI: Another speech. I...

(*HENRI begins to laugh again. TONI slaps him.*)

Quite right...quite right...what should happen if –

TONI: It won't.

HENRI: I mean –

TONI: **Won't!**

HENRI: (*HENRI contemplates this for a moment.*) Do I eat anymore?

TONI: No.

HENRI: Ahh. (*The siege is heard.*) Then how...

(*HENRI begins to laugh again. TONI slaps him.*)

Quite right...quite right...

TONI: They come. Remember they suffer enormously. They need something special. Something to sustain them through these horrors. Not emptiness.

(*The sound of many men gathering. HENRI steadies himself and stands erect. He walks to the front of the stage and directly addresses the audience.*)

HENRI: Soldiers of the faith, listen to my words.

(*A hush descends. Even the siege is silent.*)

Heaven...opened and...eyes were as a flame of fire...fire, yes, fire...clothed with a vesture dipped in blood...hear ye my defence...can't remember...we tumble and fall, tumble and fall... (*He laughs to himself.*) as if we could be turned into pillars of salt... I've seen you lot...the brutality...the sheer hatred...impressive...like artists...butchery as art...why not? The finesse of the slash...the fragility of the hack...what is the difference between the dab of the brush and the stab? Sliding scales... I don't dislike them...understand that...it's nothing personal...just – (*TONI coughs gently.*) fuck it...start again...it's fine, Toni... I'll start again...... Isn't it hot? Yer must be boilin' in that armour! (*HENRI laughs to himself.*) Not funny... I know...not funny...you must be thinking...wondering...that if you fight for the true faith...then why hasn't God shown his strength? I wonder about that, too...anything would do...a little rain for instance...how nice it would be to drink fresh water...they, the others, they would say that God fights for them... I've seen little evidence for that...maybe God can't be arsed... I mean – (*TONI coughs gently.*) I just wanna tell the truth! Only, I'm not sure...so many fragments...it's somehow right...this slaughter...natural...nothing perverted about genocide...destroy the heathen – do it with beauty...we have to accept the...no, not that...duty – to whom? For what? This sword that I carry is a holy relic...that's a lie...who decides the lie? The truth? History lies both within and without these walls...do we fight for pages in a book? Words...we fight for words...printed words...a mother's sorrow for printed words.........go annihilate the heathen...chop and hack and rip them apart...no mercy...no mercy...no mercy

(*The chant 'no mercy' is taken up by the men who we hear depart. A long spell of inactivity. TONI regards HENRI who stands as if paralysed.*)

I want the filthiest whore to piss in my face – I want to drink the bitch's piss –

(*TONI draws back a curtain to reveal a huge cross. HENRI begins to strip.*)

I want to fuck them again and again pounding them with my cock spraying my cum on their faces making others lick the mess up again and again –

(*HENRI is now naked. TONI steps up to HENRI and pulls him toward the cross. Slowly TONI ties HENRI to the cross.*)

I want four Turkish soldiers to fuck my arse until it bleeds forcing me to swallow their loads while others continue fucking me choking me with hatred and lust ripping me open without mercy –

(*TONI produces a large hammer and some nails. He begins to crucify HENRI who screams through the words.*)

I want to suck the cocks of dogs and have them tear at my skin in their frenzy wild animals gouging red chunks of my meat and feasting on my still living body –

(*HENRI's wounds bleed freely. TONI pins HENRI's feet to the cross.*)

I want to wank while horses trample me again and again cumming over my bloodied mashed body seeing my broken bones poking through the torn skin –

(*TONI sits down to admire his handiwork. HENRI continues to babble and bleed. TONI produces a bottle of wine and some food. He eats and drinks whilst watching HENRI.*)

I want my cock cut off and shoved into my mouth and someone force me to chew it and swallow it bit by bit and someone to stick hot needles into my balls two three inches long –

(*TONI begins to laugh.*)

I want to be buried in the city's cess-pit and have everyone come and shit on me shit on me shit on me –

(*LASCARIS enters.*)

LASCARIS: Mother of Christ!

(*TONI attempts to get up but LASCARIS quickly runs him through and kills him. LASCARIS wanders up to the babbling HENRI and stares at him.*)
You stupid fuck!
(*LASCARIS stabs HENRI just below the ribs in his fury. LASCARIS storms out.*)

Scene Ten

(*The scene starts with HENRI still crucified. He oversees the action, silent, but a presence. The stage is empty. Suddenly there is a shower of heads. Many are mutilated. They roll around obscenely. SIMON enters. He is filthy, derranged, and still wearing female clothes. The doll is broken but tied around his waist like a belt. He sees the heads and begins to kick some. Others he picks up and kisses. With some he forces his tongue down their gaping mouths. All the while he gibbers and laughs. He finally finds JOSEPH's head. SIMON sits and examines it. With a smile on his face SIMON pulls up his dress and begins to fuck JOSEPH's head. He moans and dribbles like a crazed animal. ANNA enters. She gingerly picks her way through the heads until she stands next to SIMON. She watches him.*)

ANNA: The trouble…it's as if you're a child again…but that would be to insult children…heads now, is it? Whose it that?
(*SIMON stops and shows ANNA JOSEPH's head.*)
Oh, so…
(*SIMON giggles and gibbers some more. He pats the head and makes cooing sounds to it. ANNA regards the head.*)
Give me a tooth.
(*SIMON forces open the mouth and pulls out a tooth. It makes a crunching sound. He gives ANNA the tooth.*)
White…so perfectly white…
(*ANNA reveals her bracelet.*)
Here is another one I shall have to have mounted. It will go well with the others.
(*SIMON gibbers.*)

Get up now...they say the relief has been spotted...help has arrived...the Turks flee...we are saved...time to rebuild...come now, darling.
(*Like a child holding on to its mother's hand, SIMON stands and is led off stage. The lights dim and all that we can see is the darkening cross.*)

The End

ANGEL OF MONS

Characters

JOHN

BRAD

DIDIER

HENSMAN

THE SARGE

ANGELIQUE

JESUS

CAPTAIN

BERT

GABRIEL

SOLDIER 1

SOLDIER 2

Angel of Mons was first performed by Concussion Productions at the White Bear Theatre, London, on Tuesday 11 May 2004, with the following cast:

JOHN, Gary Abrahams

BRAD, Steve Buchanon

SOLDIER 1, Wayne Cleworth

DIDIER, Nick Gale

HENSMAN, Jo Hammett

THE SARGE, Mark Healey

SOLDIER 2, Peter Henderson

ANGELIQUE, Katie Keady

JESUS, Tunde Makinde

SOLDIER 2, Sean McAleese

CAPTAIN, Paul Murthwaite

BERT, James O'Donnell

GABRIEL, Tom Woodman

Directed by Vincent Adams

ACT ONE

Scene One

A colossal artillery bombardment begins. The bombardment is earsplittingly loud and shakes the theatre with its violence. It continues for longer than the audience expect, disorientating them. The darkness of the theatre is punctuated by piercing flashes of light at odd moments. Just as the audience can take no more, THE SOLDIERS rush in. It is important that THE SOLDIERS adlib to convey the sense of danger, energy, and chaos. Their words will almost certainly be drowned out anyway, but those words that are heard should refer to the setting up of the defensive line, the machine guns, their terror, excitement, etc. They should be confused, occasionally discharging their weapons aimlessly. Some cower, whilst others try to organise themselves; one or two are hit by flying shrapnel, they fall and are either tended to or not. The bombardment continues through this grotesque pantomime. Smoke begins to billow through the theatre, adding to the sense of confusion and fear. As the whole scene becomes too much for all involved, GABRIEL appears. GABRIEL wears a long white robe and a sword and belt. He walks slowly toward THE SOLDIERS, who have not seen him. When GABRIEL stands amongst THE SOLDIERS, facing the German lines, he draws out his sword, and rather dramatically, flourishes it at the Germans. He seems to shout out words, which aren't heard, and somehow, he appears to glow amidst the gloom. Amazingly, the bombardment peters out quickly; indeed, the gloom is also lifted, and a twilight of sorts descends. The silence is broken only by the natural sounds of the theatre and the audience. GABRIEL stands completely still. After an eternity, THE SOLDIERS begin, tentatively, to stir. At first THE SOLDIERS concern themselves only with their immediate welfare: they tend to the wounded, look out across to the Germans, reload, organise the line, etc. Suddenly, BERT, who is lying next to the standing GABRIEL, looks up and notices him.

BERT: Fuck me old goat!

(A farcical moment occurs when all THE SOLDIERS freeze and regard GABRIEL, open-mouthed. GABRIEL soon becomes self-conscious, and breaks his statue-like appearance, by smiling at BERT. BERT, dazed, grins back. Suddenly, BRAD leaps up, and rugby tackles GABRIEL to the ground.)

BRAD: You stupid limey prick – wanna get your head blown off?

GABRIEL: *(Shaken and attempting to get up.)* Dignifiedfully I –

BRAD: *(Struggling with GABRIEL.)* Jesus, what's up with you?

GABRIEL: My robe – stained –

BRAD: Huns ain't finished yet – more of that stuff to come –

GABRIEL: Misunderstand n wrongingly –

BERT: Keep down, mate –

SOLDIER 1: 'E's gotta fuckin' sword –

SOLDIER 2: Christ, a toff, is he?

JOHN: Bloody sightseer –

BRAD: A what?

BERT: Civvie – theys come to get a look at the front –

SOLDIER 3: Tell 'im to piss off –

SOLDIER 4: 'As 'e got got any backy?

GABRIEL: Gentlemen, words of wonder, of God –

BERT: Oh, fuck me: a bible basher –

SOLDIER 1: Shoulda left him, Canada –

SOLDIER 4: Got sum backy?

SOLDIER 3: Look at 'is fuckin' 'air –

SOLDIER 2: A sodomite! A toff –

BRAD: Alright, lads, keep it down. We're supposed to be keeping a look out.

BERT: I think the Hun's kippin' down fur the evenin' –

JOHN: Maybe we can stand down –

SARGE: *(From offstage, but entering quickly.)* Right, you shower of shits, wha's the sit rep?

SOLDIER 1: Theys fucked off, Sarge –

SOLDIER 2: 'N' we've picked up a toff –

SARGE: Yer wha'?

BRAD: This...gentleman, seems to be a bit lost –

SOLDIER 4: Backy!

SARGE: Shut up, Grady. (*To GABRIEL.*) You! Wotcha doin' 'ere?

GABRIEL: (*Trying to stand and brush off the mud from his robe.*) The skies are red and truth rolls as smoke –

SARGE: Wha'?

BRAD: (*Brandishing the sword.*) He had a sword too –

SARGE: A sword! Who the fuck are yer? Where did you get this, then?

GABRIEL: In such fury, shakingly they gaped –

SARGE: I'll give yer – (*Shouts offstage.*) Captain –

BRAD: Come on, Sarge, he may be confused, but he's done no harm –

SOLDIER 3: Watch 'im – a toff –

SARGE: Arrest 'im –

SOLDIER 4: Backy!

GABRIEL: No longer stay outside to live within –

BERT: 'E's gotta be mad – look at tha' clobba –

BRAD: Give him a break, Sarge –

SARGE: Fuck you, Canada. Don' brin' any of your new world shit 'ere, right?

BRAD: Jesus –

GABRIEL: (*Animated.*) Inside, eyes looking n twist n searchingly find...nothing –

SARGE: (*Affecting a more formal tone.*) I'm sure you do, sir, but you can't be 'ere, (*Shouts offstage.*) Captain!

SOLDIER 1: 'Ere, Sarge, 'e may be a spy –

SOLDIER 2: Dressed like tha'?

SOLDIER 3: Fuck off, a toff, –

BRAD: You can't just arrest him –

SARGE: I told yer at shut up! Right, get 'im up –

JOHN: If we do that, the Hun will blow his, and our, heads off –

SARGE: Well... (*Lost for words.*)

BERT: You could arrest 'im on yer knees –

BRAD: Dear God –

SOLDIER 1: Or bent over, like –

SOLDIER 3: Too late, 'e's standin' now –

SARGE: Get 'im down –

GABRIEL: (*Whilst being wrestled to the ground by BRAD.*) You will see the silence, groaning silence –

BRAD: We're going nowhere fast here –

SOLDIER 4: Check for sum bleedin' backy, will yer?

SARGE: I'll fuck yer in a' minute, Grady –

BERT: Anyways, 'e's all dressed in white – a perfect fuckin' target for them snipers –

SARGE: Who's got a spare coat?

SOLDIER 1: Bollocks!

SARGE: All right then, you two, go an' bury Thompson – 'e's by that fuckin' 'uge shell 'ole over there –

SOLDIER 1: Oh, fuckin' 'ell, Sarge –

SARGE: Do it, 'n' Bert, you take Thompson's clothes off – 'e won't be needin' 'em now, will 'e?

BERT: Why me?

SARGE: Just do it!

(*BERT, SOLDIER 1 and SOLDIER 2 exit.*)

Right, when theys get back, clothe this fucker 'n' bring 'im over to HQ – got tha' Canada?

BRAD: Yes, Sarge –

(*The SARGE exits.*)

You all right, mate?

GABRIEL: And souls fell like dewdrops of crystal, men wailed, n all around answers lay scattered – talking in the colour of bruises –

BRAD: Don't you worry, they'll soon be talking to you –

SOLDIER 3: 'Ere, Canada, you ain't really gonna take 'im to the captain, is yer?

SOLDIER 4: Yeah, fuck 'em – this ol' geezer seems alright ta me –

SOLDIER 3: 'N' tha's a nice sword – fetch a' pretty penny, tha' will –

BRAD: You leave this sword alone – all of you –

JOHN: Well, you going to take him in?

BRAD: Nah, can't be bothered if the truth be known –

JOHN: Well, the Sarge is so fucking stupid he'll bound to forget –

SOLDIER 4: Look, fur Pete's sake, 'as 'e got any friggin' backy or not?

(*BERT enters with a uniform.*)

BERT: Fuck me, Thompson don't smell any betta dead –

BRAD: Here we go – you better put these on –

(*BERT hands GABRIEL the clothes. GABRIEL tries to stand up, but BRAD pulls him back down by grabbing his robe. The robe tears.*)

No, you·don't – put them on lying down, we all have to –

GABRIEL: My robe – contaminated –

BERT: Propa fuss pot, in 'e?

JOHN: Probably best if you put the uniform over the robe – keep you warm that way –

GABRIEL: (*Struggling with the uniform.*) What do you do to me?

(*A huge barrage erupts. THE SOLDIERS and GABRIEL all throw themselves to the ground. The noise increases until the blackout.*)

Scene Two

A horrendous explosion. A man screaming in pain. We see a DYING SOLDIER lying twisted amongst the mud and debris. Unbearable agony. JOHN enters.

JOHN: S'alright, take it easy –

SOLDER: (*Hysterical.*) Muther of Christ... 'elp me!

JOHN: (*Trying to attend to the SOLDIER's wounds.*) I'll call the medics lie still lie still –

SOLDIER: Me legs can' feel cold cold blue cold –

(*The SOLDIER screams in agony. JOHN gives up trying to attend to the SOLDIER, and instead takes out his sketch book. JOHN begins to sketch the SOLDIER – especially his wounds.*)

Don' let us die please not me please not die –

JOHN: (*Sketching furiously.*) You'll be fine just don't move!

SOLDIER: Can' die nippas wife can' die –

    (*The SOLDIER howls in pain and twists and heaves.*)

JOHN: Christ sakes lie still!

SOLDIER: (*Pulls out a blood stained letter.*) Send 'is fur us always carried it fings couldn' say 'ad to write it –

    (*Another howl of pain. JOHN takes the letter with disgust.*)

JOHN: Yes...of course.

    (*JOHN looks around and throws the letter into a shell-hole. He continues to sketch.*)

SOLDIER: I'm the last firty of us gone village pub will seem empty when it's over –

    (*More screaming pain. When the attack is over, the SOLDIER notices that JOHN is distracted.*)

    What'cha doin'?

JOHN: (*Concentrating hard.*) Filling in time before the medics get here just rest lie still –

SOLDIER: Yous aight called 'em yet...

    (*More unbearable pain. The SOLDIER begins to breath eharder and harder.*)

    'Elp me –

JOHN: (*Irritated.*) Just lie still please –

SOLDIER: (*Very agitated.*) What'cha fuckin' doin'?

JOHN: Hush hush now. (*Lowers his sketch book down for a moment and looks into the SOLDIER's eyes.*) Your eyes –

SOLDIER: Wha'?

JOHN: Your eyes –

SOLDIER: Wha's wron' with 'em?

JOHN: I need to see your eyes – look at me let me swirl around your eyes!

SOLDIER: Listen –

JOHN: Do you trust me?

SOLDIER: Wha'?

JOHN: I can see through your eyes – intently – everything – opaque soul –

SOLDIER: Please, mister, 'elp us!

JOHN: Fadingly flaying this flesh-stuff drowning this muscle-slime ripping death emerges –

SOLDIER: (*Attempts to get up.*) Wha' the fuck?

(*JOHN pushes the SOLDIER down again. The SOLDIER screams. JOHN continues to sketch.*)

JOHN: For God sakes man lie still you almost ruined the bloody picture! Don't move your gut – hanging there red-glowing scarlet-sparkling as if horror could articulate pull it more a bit more reveal its honesty with those eyes –

(*In a panic to get away from JOHN, the SOLDIER lunges to his right. The effort nearly causes him to loss consciousness. Instead he howls and howls. JOHN, clearly annoyed, pulls the SOLDIER back into position. JOHN slaps the SOLDIER.*)

Stay still! Look at me!

SOLDIER: Gut 'angin' out? (*Sudden realisation.*) Gonna die …

(*The SOLDIER, now hysterical with fear, tries to get away, but becomes more and more exhausted. His screams eventually become weaker and weaker, but not before DIDIER arrives.*)

DIDIER: I am here, *mon camarade* –

(*DIDIER spots JOHN. A confused pause.*)

Have you not helped this man?

(*Another pause.*)

I said –

JOHN: Heard you!

DIDIER: But, then –

JOHN: Heard you!

DIDIER: You should –

JOHN: Ethics certainly have their place, but exactly now they hinder confound distract so kindly fuck off before I shove this pencil up your arse...

(*DIDIER regards JOHN.*)

DIDIER: The artist!

JOHN: Oh, how tedious! An autograph now!

(*DIDIER ignores JOHN and rushes to the SOLDIER. DIDIER shakes his head when he sees the wounds. The SOLDIER is slipping away fast – very quiet and still now.*)

You couldn't just move his face toward me, could you?

(*DIDIER ignores JOHN. The SOLDIER seems to deteriorate.*)

You see useless to –

DIDIER: I'll make you eat that fucking pencil in a minute!
(*JOHN shrugs and returns to sketching. The SOLDIER dies in a gurgle of blood.*)

JOHN: (*Looks at the drawing for a moment or two, then screws it up.*) Wasn't right anyway. Missed it…again!
(*DIDIER sits back, head bowed.*)

DIDIER: (*After a passage of contemplation.*) You cunt.

JOHN: And that is French for what, precisely?

DIDIER: He's one of yours! I could understand it if he –

JOHN: What do you know about understanding?

DIDIER: I know you let him die in great pain, alone, scared, without hope –

JOHN: What hope! He's dead ain't he? He was always going to die – for fuck sakes, you see the wounds, don't you?

DIDIER: Pride –

JOHN: Bollocks! In this festering hole?

DIDIER: – for the dying and dead –

JOHN: You stupid fuck! That's exactly what – Pride! That picture could have been just maybe – the moment of spinning death – capture that – fantasy! how could it be? 'Death emerges' – grunting and heaving and screaming – his death, learnt something, art –

DIDIER: Changes nothing –

JOHN: – art –

DIDIER: Changes nothing –

JOHN: – exposes the –

DIDIER: Nothing at all –

JOHN: Shut the fuck up!

DIDIER: In this inferno –

JOHN: Art is valuable –

DIDIER: – the smashing bones –

JOHN: – and furthermore –

DIDIER: – the spraying blood –

JOHN: – a social duty to record –

DIDIER: – the slicing steel rain –

JOHN: – art records –

DIDIER: – and all you do –
JOHN: – and transmits –
DIDIER: – is paint!
JOHN: – the pain!
DIDIER: Pain? Pain! What do you know about pain?
JOHN: I'm an artist!
DIDIER: Then you know nothing – prick!
> (*A huge explosion nearby. Both DIDIER and JOHN duck at the closeness of it. After a pause, men holler and scream.*)

JOHN: (*Looking up at the sound.*) Christ! (*JOHN notices that DIDIER holds his chest as if in pain.*) You hit?
DIDIER: No – old wound – must have split open again –
JOHN: Let me see –
DIDIER: No –
JOHN: Let me see!
> (*DIDIER, resigned, opens his tunic to reveal a dirty, grubby bandage. It has fresh blood on it.*)

Peel away the bandage –
DIDIER: Look, I –
JOHN: I have a fresh dressing...now, peel away the bandage...
> (*Slowly, and in agony, DIDIER peels away the bandage which has stuck to his wound.*)

I see – split again – yes – I see – split-red-blood flowing – and cream-pus – shades of yellow – it stinks – *eau de* charnel house – pus bubblingly and frothingly alive...let me draw it –
DIDIER: Now look –
JOHN: Look at me – into my eyes – look!
DIDIER: I... I...
JOHN: Sit still...yes?
> (*DIDIER glares for a moment, but relents, nodding his head. Full of energy now, JOHN hastily produces his pencil and paper and begins to draw. Shells land near-by. Time passes. DIDIER softly begins to cry.*
> *Blackout.*)

IAIN LANDLES

Scene Three

*Gunfire resounds throughout – both artillery and machine guns.
THE SOLDIERS come streaming in, obviously in retreat. They are
scared, exhausted, dirty, and confused. They seem lost. JOHN enters,
shouting out orders.*

JOHN: To the left! Secure the left! Get down, over there!
    Keep up the firing! Take aim, for Christ sakes! Pick your
    targets! Pick your targets!
    (*THE SOLDIERS dig in and fight back. The gunfire lessens.*)
    Where's Canada? Who's seen Canada?
SOLDIER 1: I sees 'im go down –
SOLDIER 2: Nah, 'e wos runnin' fur 'is life –
DIDIER: (*Entering.*) The Germans are by the wood – direct
    your fire there –
JOHN: Fuck off! Don't need no orders from you –
DIDIER: Give cover for Canada – look, Canada's coming –
JOHN: Mother of Christ! He's carrying someone! Right,
    you lot – rapid fire – cover the man – begin rapid fire –
    (*THE SOLDIERS begin to fire and within a moment or
    two BRAD enters, carrying a WOUNDED SOLDIER. THE
    SOLDIERS cheer and continue firing. DIDIER tends to the
    WOUNDED SOLDIER. The action dies down.*)
    Cease firing! Cease firing! Oi, Jenkins!
    (*A calm descends.*)
    You're a bloody hero! Going back like that – a bloody
    hero! They'll give you a medal for that!
BRAD: (*Looks up – he is terrified.*) S'like bellowing browns
    heaving and the sky uttering sliver shrieks twisting the
    way merry-go-round –
JOHN: Steady, son –
BRAD: (*Grabs hold of JOHN's shoulders.*) The precision of
    silence sliming exhaustion and purity swamped in green
    groans of terror –
JOHN: Get a grip, man –
BRAD: I... I...drowned in a cacophony of sterility, no –
    I...spoke to the bursting colours, and...they were
    empty...

96

(*JOHN slaps BRAD, hard, brutal.*)

JOHN: Don't take it away – don't you dare take it away!
(*Silence flitters by.*)

DIDIER: No good, he's dead.
(*THE SOLDIERS and DIDIER stare at the WOUNDED MAN. The SARGE runs on stage, furious.*)

SARGE: Get up yer lazy shits! This ain't a fuckin' woman's picnic!
(*THE SOLDIERS are a flurry of activity.*)
Canada! Is this yer doin', yer lazy shit!

JOHN: Sarge, Canada went back and rescued Blacky from the Hun. On his own! Went back into that –

SARGE: Did 'e now? Abandoning 'is post, eh?

JOHN: A fucking hero, he is –

SARGE: Bollocks! Oi, Canada. Get these men movin'!

BRAD: Need rest...

SARGE: Wha'?

BRAD: The men need rest. Jesus, man, they just run for their lives, give them a minute.

SARGE: Yer thin' the 'un is gonna give us a minute? Get these fuckers on their feet 'n' outta 'ere!

DIDIER: What about this man?

SARGE: Grab 'is tags 'n' leave 'im to the crows –

BRAD: What is your problem?

SARGE: Do it or I'll 'ave you, lumberjack –

BRAD: I ain't a fucking lumberjack, you limey piece of shit!
(*BRAD moves to hit the SARGE. JOHN intervenes.*)

JOHN: Damn it, Canada –

SARGE: Go on 'it me, lumberjack –

BRAD: Cunt –
(*BRAD tries to level his gun at the SARGE, but JOHN grapples with him. At that same moment, the CAPTAIN enters, followed by GABRIEL.*)

CAPTAIN: S-S-Sergeant! Why are these men still stationary? M-M-Move them forward toward the wood –

SARGE: Forward?

CAPTAIN: You h-h-heard me, man, get this lot moving!

GABRIEL: Understand, O son of man; for at the time of the end shall be the vision –

CAPTAIN: And who is he? He follows me around talking utter d-d-drivel!

SARGE: 'E's a civvie, sir.

CAPTAIN: In a uniform? Get r-r-rid of him, sergeant, and move these men – forward!

SARGE: Yessir! (*The CAPTAIN exits.*) Right, yer 'eard the man, get crackin'!

(*THE SOLDIERS begin to cautiously move forward and exit the stage.*)

GABRIEL: He does not understand, for it is –

SARGE: Shut up, you scum! Why don' yer just fuck off!

GABRIEL: My work is here –

SARGE: Right then, bury tha' fucker! Now!

(*The SARGE exits, and GABRIEL is confused. He spots BRAD and tries to stop him as he passes him.*)

BRAD: Not now, you ponce! Can't you see that? Not now!

(*BRAD pushes GABRIEL who falls over and on to the WOUNDED SOLDIER. GABRIEL is covered in the man's blood.*)

GABRIEL: Blood...blood...and the moon was turned into blood and...

(*GABRIEL begins to cry silently. HENSMAN enters. Silence.*)

HENSMAN: Are you hurt?

GABRIEL: (*Looks up.*) Minute by minute, as if hurt came raining down-down upon you...

HENSMAN: I see...

GABRIEL: I am the mouth of God, come here to spread the message: to prepare for His coming and salvation awaits those who listen –

HENSMAN: For those who don't?

GABRIEL: Hell... I suppose...

HENSMAN: Look around you.

GABRIEL: Misunderstandingly futile.

HENSMAN: Who are you?

GABRIEL: Gabriel.

HENSMAN: They do this, Gabriel, to kill the future. Know this – that is all.

GABRIEL: Do you have a shovel? To bury this man?

HENSMAN: No, sorry.

GABRIEL: Then how will...

(*Silence.*)

HENSMAN: You were crying...

GABRIEL: Would you sit by me a while? Just a while.

(*HENSMAN looks around and then nods, sitting besides GABRIEL.*)

I find it funny how I can be so lonely amidst such frenzied fear, as if I were falling into time.

HENSMAN: You talk funny.

GABRIEL: And dress, apparently.

HENSMAN: You should go home, this suffering...needless.

GABRIEL: Your eyes!

HENSMAN: (*Trying to look away.*) What?

GABRIEL: My, your eyes! Please, let me look, please.

HENSMAN: (*Slowly turning to face GABRIEL.*) What is wrong with them?

GABRIEL: Such...harmony...yet they sing...fractiously blessed –

HENSMAN: Cursed –

GABRIEL: Blessed. And colours, prisms of reflections of love and perfection. Purity! Purity of reflection –

HENSMAN: Love? What do I know of love?

GABRIEL: Shines,...and...loneliness...missing again...and...this blue cold...everything is blue cold, even the living –

HENSMAN: I must go –

GABRIEL: Kiss me!

HENSMAN: Now look –

GABRIEL: Envelop me with your colours...for a while...just a while...

(*HENSMAN tries to get up, GABRIEL grabs HENSMAN and leans forward and they kiss – violently. Silence flutters by and HENSMAN exits. GABRIEL howls. Blackout.*)

Scene Four

ANGELIQUE is discovered washing clothes in a bucket. Distantly, the guns sound. ANGELIQUE seems oblivious to the world. She hums and talks to herself.

ANGELIQUE: Amidst the morning they came
    Bugles and smoke
    Tramp tramp tramping
    And the hugeness of colours
    (*She sings.*)
    In the cutting black, my darling,
    The cutting black
    They have stolen the stars
    And fucked us in the arse!
    (*She laughs.*)
    No matter, they said, no matter
    When they took her away
    Mother, darling, mother
    Away and still the smoke swirls
    And swirls and swirls
    (*She stops suddenly and stares at the ground.*)
    No more
    (*HENSMAN enters. ANGELIQUE stares at HENSMAN. A silence of sorts.*)
HENSMAN: I had thought that the bodies that choke the stream would make excellent stepping stones – that's what it is – stepping stones to the future. Only, one of the bodies, a young German, I think, possibly not, but a grey uniform all the same, I supposed that only...his body was not so firm and when I trod on it my boot went straight through his stomach. Now, I may be dry, but my boot is filled with rotting guts and maggots and filth as such I would never have dreamed of, and all the while why don't you fucking react to this?
    (*ANGELIQUE regards HENSMAN.*)
ANGELIQUE: You are not a man
    (*HENSMAN stands astonished.*)

HENSMAN: I need something from
you...just...something...

ANGELIQUE: When they first came
Desolate noises and silences
Searched and search did they
But there were no children
Only the prams left behind
In an old tool shed
With a leaking roof

HENSMAN: Christ, I'm tired. May I sit?

ANGLEIQUE: It is pointless to steal from me
Quite pointless
For though I cannot stop you
You will be dead soon
And I shall steal back innocently
What you stole guiltily

HENSMAN: Just rest.

ANGELIQUE: I wash my father's clothes
Quite pointless
Despite the filthy blood
The yellow smells and jagged lies
Standards yes standards
Standards
In the mire

HENSMAN: Is he an officer?

ANGELIQUE: Quite the contrary
French...more or less
A doctor now a servant
Tipsy-topsy-war-fall-down

HENSMAN: I have seen him! He cares for the wounded
soldiers. Yes, yes, I do believe I have seen him. A good
man.

ANGELIQUE: You are not a man

HENSMAN: You say that without –

ANGELIQUE: When they took Jan
Despite his struggles
Oh how he struggled
He cried

Why I ask myself why cry
Why do men cry
HENSMAN: Was Jan your brother, boyfriend?
ANGELIQUE: Let us say that we would have forty years
After the marriage naturally
Forty years yet what with
Sleep work shitting illness
Only ten years together
Ten yet even then there is
Arguments worries other people
The inevitable children
Say two months together
Two months
Why cry over two months
HENSMAN: Happiness?
ANGELIQUE: Two months in a life
Short change hole in the sock
HENSMAN: My child died – horribly – gasping for air in
water – pawing grabbing for air in water cold black
water no air – her short life spinning out before her
terrified eyes – two months, two months –
ANGELIQUE: Still
HENSMAN: I should blow your fucking brains out trample
your face in shit on your ashes – two months!
ANGELIQUE: Yes but think about how many
Months years
Of
Hurt misery fear
She has been saved from
HENSMAN: Miss her, that's all –
ANGELIQUE: I know
I have no fear that you will
Molest even rape me
None at all
HENSMAN: Why?
ANGELIQUE: You are not a man
HENSMAN: No, not at all…

(*The guns grow louder. ANGELIQUE washes and hums,
HENSMAN stares at the ground.
Blackout.*)

Scene Five

*THE SOLDIERS sit, exhausted. They are quiet, tending to
themselves, and they ignore the distant sound of guns. GABRIEL
sits among them, but even he is distant, lost in his own thoughts.
BRAD cleans his gun, occasionally stopping to listen to the guns.
BERT enters.*

BERT: Nah good, 'e's not there.

BRAD: Tom, you sure you saw him?

SOLDIER: Aye, by the tree.

BERT: Well, even the fuckin' tree is gone – musta been
  blown t' bits...

BRAD: Mark him down as absent.

GABRIEL: Shone like blue starlight n achingly with a
  terrible serenity drifted did he into arms n forever...

BERT: Cheerful fuck, aint 'e?

  (*The SARGE and CAPTAIN enter. THE SOLDIERS are a
  flurry of activity.*)

SARGE: Right, yer –

CAPTAIN: S-S-S'alright, Sergeant. Leave them be.

SARGE: Very well, sir. Sit! (*THE SOLDIERS sit down,
  puzzled.*) Right you buggers, listen up! The captain 'as
  decided t' share sumthin' with yers. Captain?

CAPTAIN: T-T-T-Thank you. Men, brothers, may I say;
  Brothers, we have our f-f-f-first medal! (*Silence.*) I have b-
  b-b-been awarded the DSM! The sergeant, here was
  witness for me and proposed me to the general. T-T-T-
  The medal, as they say, is in the post.

  (*The CAPTAIN chuckles and the SARGE smiles. Another
  silence. The SARGE, angered, steps forward.*)

SARGE: A'right then, give the man a cheer!

(*THE SOLDIERS give three half-hearted cheers. The CAPTAIN, pleased, smiles at them. The SARGE seethes with anger.*)

CAPTAIN: A f-f-f-few words, sergeant?

SARGE: It's 'bout rippin' their eyes out 'n' hackin' 'n' slicin' poundin' the fuckers stampin' 'n' stampin' on 'em till the ground runs red 'n' fury tearin' their skin clawin' at their throats no quarter no mercy 'n' all the while 'ate 'n' 'ate fur wha' they's did 'n' wha's they's to yet do shoot the animals club the scum gouge 'n' kill 'em kill 'em kill 'em 'til there ain't nothing' left annihilate 'em come on yer fuckas kill 'em kill 'em kill 'em
(*Most of THE SOLDIERS take up the SARGE's refrain, and soon get worked up. Only BRAD, JOHN and GABRIEL remain still. THE SOLDIERS clap and cheer. The CAPTAIN seems pleased.*)

CAPTAIN: Well done, s-s-s-sergeant. Carry on.
(*The CAPTAIN exits. The SARGE glares at THE SOLDIERS, before following the CAPTAIN.*)

BRAD: (*Looking at THE SOLDIERS.*) Don't take long – men to beasts in the flicker of a flag. Jesus, what's the point?

JOHN: So it's true, then. The captain took your medal, Brad.

BERT: Just like toffs!

BRAD: Didn't want no medal anyhow, boys.

JOHN: But, for fuck's sake –

BRAD: Leave it, John, it's over now.

JOHN: Leave it! He's got your medal! The shit can't even speak right let alone save a man!

BERT: 'e's right, Canada. 'em captain's ain't too brave. Don't feel good givin' 'em medals fur nought.

BRAD: Didn't I just see you screaming like a banshee? You're just like them, Bert.

BERT: Leave it ou'! Nuthin' like 'im.

BRAD: You Brits! Up the king and all that. Watcha fighting for, Bert?

BERT: 'em 'uns! I've 'eard theys even kill babies. Now tha' ain't right, is it?

BRAD: No, but what are you really fighting for? God, the
   king, empire?

BERT: Wanna make thin's...safe, like –

BRAD: Christ sakes!

JOHN: Leave him, Canada. He's got a right to –

BRAD: To what? Die like a trussed up pig!

BERT: Now listen here, son –

BRAD: You listen, son. Them 'toffs' don't give a fuck about
   you and the boys – you're offal to them. Do as you're
   told, march here, fight there, die right now. Is that what
   it's about? You're fucking pigmeat!

JOHN: And you? You came all this way for what? Wanna
   win a medal?

BRAD: After this carnage – a new order – like a snow globe
   – it all gets shaken up – and what floats down ain't the
   same –

JOHN: Dear Christ, not that again –

BRAD: Why not? You got something better?

BERT: Pride, mate, 'n' tradition –

BRAD: Bollocks!

JOHN: It's art that will change the world –

BRAD: Here we go –

JOHN: Not your manifestos –

BRAD: Right, a painting will stop the Hun –

JOHN: Don't be fucking stupid – of course not –

BRAD: Then you're full of shit –

JOHN: The principles of art – the things we learn –

BERT: Sounds crap to me –

JOHN: Which artist ever exploited anyone?

BRAD: And who owns the art?

JOHN: That's just greed –

BRAD: Your idealism is as weak as your paint – it washes
   out!

JOHN: If the world thought as we do –

BRAD: Now that is fucking crap: imagine this lot actually
   thinking –

JOHN: If they could believe –

BRAD: They believe in nothing –

BERT: Tha' ain't true –

BRAD: Go on then, Bert, me old mucker, what do you
believe in?

BERT: Decency!

BRAD: Tell that to the dead –

JOHN: You're just a snob like the captain –

BRAD: Fuck you –

JOHN: Replace one set of scum with another –

BERT: Nuthin' wrong in decency –

BRAD: Get it straight, you fuckers, no one believes in
anything, anymore –

JOHN: They could do though, it's up to us to –

BRAD: Crap –

JOHN: Imagine it, though –

BRAD: Never happen! Who could be arsed to actually
believe in anything?

GABRIEL: Talk they strangefully whispers of love whispers
of hate the glowing dawn peeling away the vitality of
betrayal the desire of hypocrisy stand naked thus truthful
lies shades of grey flecks of passion and all the while the
rhythm and beat of purity tainted innocence one more
time Oh I have seen sterile blindness forcefully coerce
them swamped drowning still they cry lust earth rising
tumbling they sell the piece for peace hanging caught
the wire pinned wriggling the whole is fragmented and I
slide slide slide clarity a little worse for wear (*GABRIEL
produces a bayonet.*) blood 'tis fashion an accessory and we
shall wear it as pridefulingly as we can strike for honesty
(*GABRIEL slowly pushes the bayonet into his eye. It is a
deliberate, slow, brutal act. The men around him sit dazed and
shocked, still unable to react.*) and blood drifted down as
snow and the stars tumbled and the books opened to
reveal...absence

(*GABRIEL lurches forward in agony. BRAD rushes to him
and pulls the bayonet out. GABRIEL screams and passes
out. The men look at GABRIEL, then at one another.
Blackout.*)

Scene Six

The SARGE sits cleaning his gun. Artillery is heard distantly. The SARGE seems preoccupied: he cleans his gun in an automatic way. He stops and takes out a photograph from his tunic. Time passes.

SARGE: Ice black ice black the edge of all things
  (*Abruptly, the SARGE returns the photograph and begins to clean his gun again. He stares into the distance, haunted, alone. GABRIEL enters. His damaged eye sports a bloodied bandage. GABRIEL stares at the SARGE, who does not acknowledge GABRIEL's presence. Time.*)

GABRIEL: Time it shuffles old man blue's glaringly nostalgic sorrowfully angry it's not as if colours fall from it as rainbow tears – no not that just violent silence

SARGE: Still 'ere? No shell incinerate ya? Melt the skin off yer bone? Missed the stray bullet tha' plunges deeper 'n' deeper, haulin' yer screamin' soul off ta 'ell? Eh?

GABRIEL: No

SARGE: Still 'ere, then?

GABRIEL: Yes

SARGE: Who is ya?

GABRIEL: I am Gabriel, that stand in the presence of God; and am sent to speak unto thee –

SARGE: God, tha's a good un. Aye, God.

GABRIEL: He watches –

SARGE: Not all the time –

GABRIEL: He watches –

SARGE: Then 'e's a shit! Watches blind! Time blind!

GABRIEL: Time not blind a snowstorm of envelopment –

SARGE: Blindin' snow!

GABRIEL: At once here and there –

SARGE: Tumblin' chaotic dice fallin' as snow –

GABRIEL: He watches aware –

SARGE: No one watches!

GABRIEL: Foresees the slightest hurt –
  (*The SARGE leaps up and smashes GABRIEL in the face with his rifle butt. GABRIEL collapses to the ground*

screaming. The SARGE throws down his rifle and begins to brutally kick GABRIEL about the head and body.)

SARGE: Foresee tha'? 'N' tha'? Cum on where 'is 'e then? Lettin' yer down ain't 'e? Knew it was comin' 'e knew! So where 'is 'e? 'E's doin' this! 'Is makin'! 'Im not me!

(The SARGE stops and grabs the battered GABRIEL.)

'E's a bastard theys all is with their gibberin's 'n' fancy talk-talk wha' care they 'e enjoys the pain seein' us crawlin' 'n' hollerin' pain feeds 'im soft words built on pain

(The SARGE lets go of GABRIEL and then urinates on him.)

Take tha' back to 'im – message of love.

(The SARGE finishes, picks up his rifle and exits. Time flitters by and guns are heard. GABRIEL is motionless. HENSMAN enters.)

HENSMAN: Saw everything – could've helped – yes – could've helped – but no – didn't *(A silence.)* don't know why – didn't help

(HENSMAN sits on the ground and listens to the guns for a while. GABRIEL finally stirs.)

GABRIEL: You...again...

HENSMAN: Yes, again...the guns – sing. Have you noticed? Singing songs – songs of rhythm – killing rhythm –

GABRIEL: Drawn it seems –

HENSMAN: Hardly –

GABRIEL: Together –

HENSMAN: Well...

GABRIEL: I do not feel him anywhere – black stars

HENSMAN: No – nowhere –

GABRIEL: Once –

HENSMAN: No sermons – not now –

GABRIEL: He spoke white words n everywhere the green music lullaby warm
floatingly warm

(HENSMAN, with a sigh, begins to clean GABRIEL up with some rags and water. GABRIEL talks haltingly.)

Unsorry
all things fall see see the ghosts
merry-go-round of unrising n unfalling
caught
pinned
(*HENSMAN gently lifts GABRIEL into a sitting position
and continues to clean him up. GABRIEL strokes
HENSMAN's cheek.*)
Your fragmented eyes
silly eyes for being so dazzling
Here
with the tainted mud
silly
being near you with you
bathed in clear colours of fragility
HENSMAN: Enough now –
GABRIEL: In the paining n unlight
dirty stars
I remembered only
You
N trembling awfully
I have seen the unbending brilliance
Magnetic logic
N meaning
Yet I say you
Rainbow eyes
meaning beyond words
I love you
N will renounce the brilliance
For you
(*A silence where GABRIEL stares up at HENSMAN, who
ignores him. Finally.*)
HENSMAN: Love slips and slides becoming ever elusive
and in the loneliness seems as if it never existed at all. I
have abandoned love for it abandoned me. I am the void
and nothing ever leaves that enters here. I say this, for
you are clearly lost, and I cannot help you. That is all I
can give.

GABRIEL: There is always hope –

HENSMAN: No. Perversity in ambition. Love me if you wish. Flea to a dog – sometimes I will scratch, sometimes not.

GABRIEL: Brutality of ecstasy – love me –

HENSMAN: No –

GABRIEL: Love me –

HENSMAN: No…

(*HENSMAN continues to clean GABRIEL, who continues to stare up at HENSMAN. The guns sound. Time. Blackout.*)

Scene Seven

JOHN and BERT assist an ILL SOLDIER. The ILL SOLDIER appears feverish and very weak. The group stop at a huge shell hole that looks like a crater on the moon.

BERT: 'Ere yer go, son, the latrines at last!

JOHN: Christ, the smell!

BERT: (*Helping the ILL SOLDIER to take down his trousers.*) Ain't just shit down there, neither: dead horses, men, fuck know's wha'.

JOHN: How did we get this job! It's fucking dangerous! Fucking Sergeant! I'm an artist, not a fucking nurse!

BERT: Look, mate, this geezer 'ere 'as got dysentery – yer ever 'ad tha'? Fuckin' horrible, the lad can 'ardly stand. Shat 'is life awa', 'e 'as. Weak as fuck. So stop whingein' 'n' gis us a' 'and 'ere.

(*BERT and JOHN position the ILL SOLDIER at the edge of the shell hole.*)

There yer go, son. Stick yer arse over tha' lot 'n' let us know when yer done.

(*BERT and JOHN move away from the crouching ILL SOLDIER.*)

Poor fucker, the Sarge reckons 'e's malingerin'. I mean, come on, look at 'im!

JOHN: Just another deathsack in waiting.

BERT: Yer know John, yer gotta 'ave some bleedin' sympathy – we'll all in this together, yer know.

JOHN: Oh, grow up, Bert! Most of us are here 'cause we've been sent here. Not much 'solidarity' here, mate.

BERT: Be as tha' may be, now we're 'ere, we're stickin' together, like – one for all, 'n' all tha'.

JOHN: You really believe in that shit, don't you?

BERT: 'Ad this same argument before –

JOHN: But there's no such thing as being 'British' –

BERT: Me missus used to say: "Ere we go again –'

JOHN: What do you think it means to be British?

BERT: I took yer in, fed yer, 'n' yer bored the crap outta me –

JOHN: Alright, what about those who weren't 'born here', but still consider themselves 'British'?

BERT: Like who?

JOHN: The fucking Indians they're dying in hoards –

BERT: Theys ain't fuckin' British –

JOHN: What are they then?

BERT: Fuckin' foreigners –

JOHN: They're part of the Empire –

BERT: Look John, everyone knows theys ain't one of us –

JOHN: They're still fighting for us.

BERT: Yes, but –

JOHN: The 'British' are a rag-bag collection of just about every other European nation: the Danes, the Swedes, the Italians, Jesus Christ, even the fucking Germans!

BERT: I knows tha', wha' I'm sayin' is –

JOHN: It's like you're fighting against yourself –

BERT: S'like a' principle – freedom, or sumthin' –

JOHN: Don't make me laugh –

BERT: Alright, 'ow 'bout killin' the fuckin' 'un before 'e swans over ta Blighty 'n' fucks the shit outta me wife!

JOHN: So much for nationalism!

BERT: Yer know, yer just like them toffs – talk rubbish to us 'n' make us all confused – usin' big words 'n' notions, like – we don't know – whatever yer's tell us we think is right, so tha' it seems tha' everthin' is right – 'ow the fuck do wes choose?

JOHN: Instinct –

BERT: Me wife says, 'n' yer were there, right –

JOHN: Bert! This is one shitty war, yes?

BERT: Just listen –

JOHN: And no one single soldier, on either side, can do this much longer, yes?

BERT: Fair comment –

JOHN: Then what if, forgetting nationalism and all that bollocks, what if every single soldier in this war, put down his rifle and said, that's it, no more, I'm going home?

BERT: They'd 'ave a few things t' say 'bout tha' back 'ome –

JOHN: Maybe, 'Hip-hip-hoo-fucking-ray'. Bert, not another man, boy, or child hurt – imagine it, Bert. We stop fighting for maps, or names, or even 'principles'. We just use our common sense and fuck off back home.

BERT: Well, suppose so…but I wouldn't trust 'em 'uns –

JOHN: Jesus –

(*While BERT and JOHN have been talking, the ILL SOLDIER has slowly slid into the shell hole. At this point, BERT turns round to check on him and sees that he has disappeared.*)

BERT: Fuck me! Where's the lad gone?

(*Both men rush to the edge of the shell hole and look down, into it.*)

Oh, me God! 'E's sliding in –

JOHN: Don't move, mate –

BERT: Christ, 'e's nearly in it –

JOHN: Bert, have you got a rope?

BERT: Don't be fuckin' stupid –

JOHN: (*Taking off his scarf.*) Here! Mate! Grab a' hold of this –

BERT: Look! 'E's tryin'! Bit further, mate! Come on!

JOHN: He's slipping! Don't move! Just stop!

BERT: Yer 'eard the man, stop!

JOHN: Bert! He's slipping in! Up to his waist!

BERT: Fuck me! Do sumthin'!

JOHN: What!

BERT: 'Ang on, mate! 'Ang on!

> (*Both men stare transfixed at the ILL SOLDIER. The audience can tell the ILL SOLDIER's progress by the expressions on both JOHN and BERT. Time passes. Finally it is all over. Both men continue to stare, and JOHN sinks to the ground, horrified. BERT turns away and puts his head into his hands. Silence.*)

Gone! Seen it all now – a man drownin' in shit!

JOHN: His face – stared at me – those eyes – saw right through his eyes!

BERT: Wha' wes goin' tell the Sarge?

JOHN: What?

BERT: 'E'll fuckin' kill us if 'e finds out wha' happened 'ere.

JOHN: The truth –

BERT: Truth be fucked! We're supposed to look after 'im!

JOHN: I... I can't get past those eyes –

BERT: Listen, mate, I don't know wha' yer on, but I don't wanna get on the bad side of the Sarge, got it? We'll say 'e got done by a shell or sumthin'.

JOHN: His body?

BERT: Buried it, you prick!

JOHN: Tags –

BERT: Blown off 'im! Jesus, you're supposed to be smart, ain't yer?

JOHN: I... I...his eyes...

BERT: Tell yer wha', yer paint 'is fuckin' eyes 'n' I'll tell the Sarge, yes? Life goes on, mate, remember tha'.

> (*JOHN slowly nods and we Blackout.*)

Scene Eight

A horrendous barrage. Lights flash where the shells explode. Men scream in the near distance. Darkness otherwise. Gradually the barrage moves on and the light begins to rise. We hear the SARGE shout 'Expect 'em to come! Expect 'em to come!', from offstage. BERT staggers on, plainly drunk. He gibbers, alternating between laughter and complete horror. He finally falls and pulls out a virtually empty bottle. He hears the SARGE again and cowers. A WOUNDED SOLDIER crawls onstage and collapses near BERT.

BERT: (*Begins to sing.*) If the sergeant drinks your rum, never mind
And your face may lose its smile, never mind
He's entitled to a tot but not the bleeding lot
If the sergeant drinks your rum, never mind
SOLDIER: Tha'...tha' yer, Bertie?
(BERT begins to cry softly, trying to sing his song.)
'Ere, son, if tha's yer, gis us a' 'and...me bleedin' guts is 'angin' out...
(BERT ignores the WOUNDED SOLDIER and continues to drink and sing. Each explosion causes BERT to curl up a little tighter. He whimpers and howls.)
Ahh, Bert...ahh, Bert...it's alright, son, it's alright...
(BRAD enters and spots the men.)
BRAD: You guys okay?
SOLDIER: Bert's...gone...funny, like...must be 'urt...
(BRAD sees how bad the wounds are on the WOUNDED SOLDIER. He turns to BERT.)
BRAD: Bert, can you help me? Bert, listen to me –
(BRAD stops as BERT laughs. BRAD grabs BERT.)
You're drunk! Jesus Christ alive! Bert! Bert!
(BRAD slaps BERT, who responds with fear.)
BERT: Didn' mean it – didn' mean it – 'ad to fed the lass – starving' she was – starving', I'll work it off – tell me wha' it cost – I'll work it off –
(BERT bursts into tears. He sobs. BRAD holds BERT in his arms, gently rocking him.)
BRAD: It's alright, Bert, it's alright...
BERT: 'E's all around – seekin' 'n' killin' –
BRAD: What? What is, Bert?
BERT: 'Is smile – gratin' shudders –
(Whistles are heard distantly.)
BRAD: Over here! Wounded men! Over here!
(JOHN runs on and immediately kneels besides the WOUNDED SOLDIER.)

John, how bad is he? I think it's Tim – got that braiding on his kit –

JOHN: He's a fucking goner! What's the point of training us in first aid! Should have been an undertaker – would have made a fortune.

BRAD: Bert's lost it –

JOHN: (*Noticing BERT for the first time.*) What's up? Is he hit?

BRAD: Drunk.

JOHN: Oh, for fuck sakes! The Sarge is on his way over here.

BRAD: (*BRAD points to his head.*) But I don't think he's right up here. That barrage must have taken it out of him.

JOHN: Get rid of him, quick. If the Sarge comes over he'll go ape-shit! For fuck sakes, what a fucking mess!

BRAD: (*To BERT, still holding him.*) Bert, we have to get up now –

BERT: Pay yer back – promise it – pay yer back –

BRAD: Come on, mate.

(*BRAD helps BERT to his feet. BERT spots JOHN and stops.*)

BERT: Angel of death –

(*BERT, wide-eyed with fear, screams and babbles.*)

JOHN: Get him out of here!

(*BRAD literally pulls BERT off. JOHN sits down by the WOUNDED SOLDIER.*)

No hope...no hope. You lucky, pal, this is your time.

(*JOHN pulls out his sketch book and begins to draw the WOUNDED SOLDIER.*)

SOLDIER: (*Recovering.*) 'Ere, it's the bleedin' artist –

JOHN: Lie still, now – help is on the way.

SOLDIER: I've seen the state I'm in...no bleedin' way I'll be goin' 'ome...fuck, it 'urts...

JOHN: (*Inspired.*) Look, I...death, it's about death...capturing the...duty to educate the next generation –

SOLDIER: Let 'em cum 'ere for a couple of weeks –

JOHN: No, I mean...death is the standard by which we measure life...jagged death reflects life...no, I mean, look…you're dying…no hope…tripping and sliding and tumbling into death…let me capture that…death emerging…in you…feel it squirming…death alive…

SOLDIER: Tell yer wha', mate,…yer go 'n' fuck yerself…
(*JOHN slowly slips his scarf off and puts it around the neck of the WOUNDED SOLDIER. JOHN tightens his grip and begins to strangle the WOUNDED SOLDIER, who, weak with his wound, is unable to fight back. The WOUNDED SOLDIER dies horribly. Time passes. JOHN, at first excited, finally slumps back, now exhausted.*)

JOHN: Missed it…missed it…

SARGE: (*Offstage, but entering.*) But I didn't miss it.
(*JOHN starts, but realises quickly there is no where to go. He stares at the SARGE. The SARGE levels his gun at JOHN.*)
'Eard stories 'bout yer, 'course I 'ave. Everyone 'as. A cocky bastard who thinks 'e knows it all. Talkin' down to us. Like sum snob. Only yer ain't a snob, is yer, mate? Just another piece of shit like me 'n' the rest.

JOHN: Look, Sarge –

SARGE: Shut it! Yer think I'm gonna listen to some airy-fairy twat like yer? Fuck off, yer dun now, pal. Drawin' the dyin'. Like tha', do yer? Fuckin' perverted that is, mate. Perverted.

JOHN: I'm not going to argue with you, Sarge. It would be my word against yours –

SARGE: Yer think I'm gonna tell on yer? (*He laughs.*) Look 'ere, son, yer really are a twat, ain't yer? I ain't gonna let this one go, no way. Power is in the hand tha' holds it. Come 'ere!
(*Defenceless, without his gun, which lies nearby, JOHN slowly walks towards the SARGE.*)
Gotta learn, pal, the world is a 'orrible place, 'n' all 'em nightmares yer ma told yer 'bout, is true – only, they is a lot worse than yer could ever imagine –
(*Without warning, the SARGE slams his rifle into JOHN's head. JOHN falls to the ground half-unconscious and bleeding.*)

Tellin' me wha' to do.

(*The SARGE drops his gun and undoes his trousers.*)

I'll give yer art, yer fuckin' piece of shit.

(*Amongst the backdrop of an ever-increasing artillery barrage, the SARGE rapes JOHN violently. At times JOHN tries to fight back, but the SARGE punches him in the back of the head, time and again. JOHN eventually loses consciousness. The SARGE finishes and gets up, pulling up his trousers and looking down at JOHN.*)

There, now we both got our secrets, eh, pal?

(*The SARGE exits as we Blackout.*)

Scene Nine

The SOLDIERS sit in a large hollow. A couple of soldiers are watching the German positions, the rest sit around cleaning their weapons, talking, sleeping, etc. GABRIEL sits alone. He looks tired, dirty, and depressed. BRAD sits next to BERT forcing him to drink water. There is silence.

GABRIEL: Lost sight...distracted...as if looking through shattered crystals...a multiplicity of vision...each with their twists and dead-ends and the road ever climbing...picturefully erupting...unsaid...so much unsaid...lurks within...censored images... (*To the SOLDIERS, animated.*) My men, hark the foul thunder, the cacophony of clouds, the clamour of steel rain, listen to my words –

SOLDIER 1: Christ sakes, tell 'im to button it –

SOLDEIR 2: I'll fuckin' do 'im in a minute –

SOLDIER 3: 'E shouldn't even be 'ere with tha' eye –

BRAD: Alright, keep it down, lads –

GABRIEL: And the people of the prince that shall come shall destroy the city and the sanctuary; and the end thereof shall be with a flood, and unto the end of the war desolation are determined –

SOLDIER 2: (*Getting up and advancing toward GABRIEL.*) Tha's the last fuckin' straw – I'm gonna kill the shit –

BRAD: (*Intercepting the SOLDIER.*) That's enough, sit down –

SOLDIER 2: 'Ave you 'eard 'im?

BRAD: I'll sort it out – now sit down! (*SOLDIER 2 glares at GABRIEL, but obeys BRAD. BRAD sits next to GABRIEL, who has sunk back into his depressed state.*) Gabriel, you mustn't say such things, it upsets the men. They need their rest.

GABRIEL: (*Intense.*) Purpose deflected as rainbow light...and what seemed firm shakes...fragility of flowers... I am blinded by betrayal –

BRAD: Gabriel, go home, son –

GABRIEL: 'Tis all mist...vaporous...the message falsely translated... I do not speak their language –

BRAD: These men are tired, afraid, they have no time to listen to stories –

GABRIEL: They bellow to blot out their whispering souls – wilfully discordant...drown as incineration if they cannot hear the words –

BRAD: Not helping –

GABRIEL: And love...

BRAD: Love?

GABRIEL: How do you stand it?

BRAD: I don't understand, isn't love the answer?

GABRIEL: Nails in the skin – seething reds and violent blues – how the heart beatingly ignores the rhythm – love is the chaos of distraction!

BRAD: Look, son, you got to take it easy, relax, you know? Maybe I should send you down the line – get your eye fixed. What do you think?

GABRIEL: Depths beyond salvation – abandoned – a desolate place – long I fell – he will not be there – lost – all lost – still it grinds on –

BRAD: Gabriel, who was that soldier I saw you with? The one that helped you back here? Yesterday, remember? Maybe he could help.

GABRIEL: Chaos –

(*BRAD notices JOHN enter and sit down, away from the others.*)

BRAD: John, come over here, I need your help.

(*JOHN, with a great effort, gets up and comes over.*)

I've just about got Bert sober, but now Gabriel's gone funny. We've got to get him out of here.

GABRIEL: N alone

As if it's natural

Drowning

Lungs filling

Without purchase

Sliding

N no mercy

No innocence

Alone

You have no idea

JOHN: Do they still laugh at him?

BRAD: Not laughing now – more like hate.

JOHN: The splinters of hate –

BRAD: Christ, don't you start. What is up with everyone?

GABRIEL: Waiting for absence – eternity...

(*Movement. Machine guns are heard. The SOLDIERS spring into action. Each one lies at the top of the hollow, gun in hand. BRAD assumes control. JOHN sits staring at GABRIEL, who is now quietly weeping.*)

BRAD: What the hell are they firing at?

SOLDIER 1: They can't be attackin' –

SOLDIER 2: Maybe they're bored –

SOLDIER 3: 'Ere, Bert, got any of tha' rum left?

BERT: Why can't they just shut the fuck up?

SOLDIER 1: Maybe theys pissed off tha' Bert's 'ad all the booze!

(*General laughter. BERT mouths 'Fuck off' to a couple of the SOLDIERS.*)

SOLDIER 3: 'Ere, Canada, wha's tha'?

BRAD: I don't know looks like –

SOLDIER 1: Fuck me, it's Gabriel!

SOLDIER 2: Can't be – tha' twat's back there –

SOLDIER 3: But 'e's all in white –

SOLDIER 2: Not another one –

BRAD: Right, lads, whoever he is, he don't deserve to be gunned down by the Hun. Give the man support fire.
(*The SOLDIERS begin to fire back at the Germans.*)
Jesus, I can't believe he isn't hit!

SOLDIER 1: I swear 'em bullets is goin' right thru 'im!
(*GABRIEL stands up and looks toward no-man's-land.*)

JOHN: What is it? You look like you're smelling something.

SOLDIER 1: Did you see tha'? Bleedin' shell burst right next to 'im. Didn't even flinch!

BRAD: Watch out, lads, here he is. Cease fire!
(*The machine gun fire dies down. From the gloom and smoke of the battlefield emerges a figure. Like GABRIEL he is dressed in a white robe. He carries no sword. He walks to the lip of the hollow and stares down at the SOLDIERS. They stare back up at him, agog. A huge silence.*)

JESUS: (*Gently.*) All power is given unto me in heaven and earth; and lo, I am with you always, even unto the end of the world. Amen.
(*Blackout.*)

ACT TWO

Scene One

JESUS is surrounded by the SOLDIERS, JOHN, BRAD, BERT, DIDIER, and GABRIEL. They all sit, listening to JESUS. JESUS is softly spoken and appears quite comfortable.

JESUS: And Zaccerus was a renowned farmer. Everyone marvelled at his success. He would farm by the old ways and always treat field, beast, and man well and with reverence. His wares became famous for their quality and they fetched the best prices at market. A wise man, too, was he known as. Many would come to him to ask him to settle disputes – even from far away. Listen too would he to complaints from his own workers, and judge accordingly. Loved and held in high esteem; a man at peace with men and earth. A good man. Now Zaccerus had two sons – Joseph and James. Joseph was like his father in many ways – his even temperament and fair mood. He always deferred to his father in all matters, and the people loved him for working with them in the fields. James did not work in the fields. He was content to stay in the house and pore over account books and plans for increasing the yield from the fields. He became pale from want of sunlight, and the people did not know him, for always he hid and said little save to his father. Now few knew that Zaccerus would listen all night to James' schemes and plans. Not that Zaccerus agreed with any of the schemes, but solely because he loved his son, and would not insult nor upset him by dismissing him. Zaccerus was a clever man, and each scheme James proposed, Zaccerus would refute through excellent and learned discourse. James, frustrated, would not risk his father's temper, and would concede, although heavy of heart. Now Zaccerus' land was dry and the water he fed his crops and animals on came from his neighbour who

121

had a rich stream flowing across his land. Zaccerus paid
a yearly tribute to his neighbour, and a complex system
was erected to feed Zaccerus' land. James had always
bemoaned this tribute, saying that without it, Zaccerus
would be richer still. Zaccerus paid no attention to
James, for this arrangement had been successful for
many a time. One year a heavy fever overcame Zaccerus
and none but his sons where allowed near him. 'In my
weak state, perhaps death, I pass the farm to your hands,
my sons.' And with that, Zaccerus departed this earth.
Now Joseph and James used to argue over how the farm
was to be run, but Joseph, in his misery over his father's
death, allowed James the ascendancy. And James decreed
that the tribute paid to the neighbour would henceforth
be abandoned. 'How shall we water our lands?' asked
Joseph. 'I shall see to it,' replied James, 'you make
preparations for the burial of our beloved father.' And
with that James collected the men of the farm together
and bade them work with him for the memory of
Zaccerus and to a man they said 'Aye'. And James took
the men high into the mountains and his purpose was to
dam the stream and send its travel another way – that
away from the neighbour's land, and onto his land. Long
they toiled, day and night, and many a man grew weak
and ill. But still James pushed them on sensing that he
would at last have his way. It was on the seventh day that
the first man died, then another, then another, and all the
while the toil grew longer and more dangerous. 'Just
another day,' said James, but day turned into day into
day. But lo, by the third month James had dammed the
stream and rejoiced in his strength of mind. But looking
around him only three other men stood, for the rest had
died. Returning to their lands besides the stream, James
came upon annihilation, for pestilence had visited with
heavy hammer blows and only a few old women lived.
Much wailing scorched the air and death was happy for
so few lived. And the lands of Zaccerus, now watered,
fell into rot, for the crops were not tendered and the

beasts fell ill and died for the eating of the rotten crops, and James was the last, and in his agony leaped into the stream and was drowned and washed away and thus ends the story of the lands of Zaccerus.

BERT: Bleedin' 'ell, poor bastards –

SOLDIER 1: Is 'e sayin' tha' back 'ome will be fucked?

SOLDIER 2: 'Ow can it be?

SOLDIER 1: Could be tha' disease 'e talked 'bout –

JOHN: Listen to yourselves –

SOLDIER 3: Alright for you, son, you don' work on a farm –

JOHN: No, he wasn't saying that –

SOLDIER 2: Nobody mentioned anything' in me last letter –

BERT: Maybe theys all died since then –

BRAD: Futility – obvious as day –

BERT: Yer wha'?

BRAD: He wants us to stop fighting...

(*An uncomfortable pause. JESUS still appears relaxed and he looks at each man in turn.*)

JESUS: Didier. You seem distracted.

DIDIER: No, not at all. Just...

BERT: Wha' it is, man?

DIDIER: He talks sense, you should listen to him, but you won't...you'll all pig-die instead –

BRAD: That's enough. It's bad enough –

BERT: (*To JESUS.*) Yer mean, desert?

JESUS: How can you turn your back on that which you don't believe in?

SOLDIER 2: I believe in wha' we're doin' –

JESUS: (*Snarls with contempt.*) To butcher and be butchered –

BRAD: Let's all calm down –

JESUS: Look at yourselves – sheep waiting for the cull – you!

(*JESUS grabs SOLDIER 2 by the face and stares deep into his eyes.*)

Tell of the dream.

SOLDIER 2: Wha'?

JESUS: The dream...

SOLDIER 2: (*Struggling with himself.*) I... 'ow do... I...s'like a beach 'n' grey mournful sky blue wind and fury... 'n' I stand watchin'...desolate... 'n' she is there – besides me... 'n' 'old 'ands 'n' it feels as if I'll die from love, only...only I don' know who she is... 'n' when I wake...seems like black crashes into my heart...like ...

JESUS: How will you know her if they obliterate your soul in the burning mud? Even the fragility of a flower needs more than one raindrop.

(*Silence wafts past and finally.*)

SOLDIER 2: I won't fight no more...

BRAD: Now look, son –

BERT: Wha' 'bout the 'un? Is 'e gonna just fuck off?

JESUS: Brad, how often do you think about Otto?

JOHN: Who?

JESUS: And how he looked that white cold morning and the things he said and promised to do and the sadness when you watched him walk away, how often do you sigh?

JOHN: Canada? What the fuck's he talking about?

BRAD: I was there when the Jerrys came out of the line at Christmas – waving white hankies and bringing over cigars and... I couldn't believe it was Otto – met him a year before in Paris...seems like an age now...

JOHN: A friend?

BRAD: Found his body by the river...bloated and burst...head torn off... I kissed his hands and the skin stuck to my lips...

JESUS: They are shopkeepers and teachers and fathers and men. Monsters exist only in the minds of those that drive you from both sides.

(*The SOLDIERS are all confused, embarrassed, and indecisive. Shells land distantly; machine gun-fire is heard. Movement off stage and then the SARGE and the CAPTAIN enter rapidly.*)

SARGE: Right yer lot, up 'n' at 'em.

(*There is little movement, most of the men don't know what to do. BRAD stands lost in thought. JESUS and DIDIER have vanished.*)

Wha' the fuck do yer think yer doin'? I said move!

SOLDIER 2: I ain't gonna fight no more.

(*SOLDIER 2 throws down his gun. The SOLDIERS all begin to speak at once – a babble.*)

CAPTAIN: S-S-Sergeant?

BERT: (*Shouting over the rest.*) It's like this, Sarge –

(*The SARGE pulls out a revolver and without pausing shoots SOLDIER 2 in the head. Chaos, then absolute silence.*)

SARGE: The next fucker who says tha' gets it too! Got it?

(*The SOLDIERS are terrified and slowly pick up their equipment. BRAD stares at the SARGE.*)

Got a problem, lumberjack? Now fuckin' move, the lot of yer!

(*All the SOLDIERS move off, most stare at the body of SOLDIER 2. The CAPTAIN is shaking.*)

CAPTAIN: Was there... I-I-I mean... I-I-I –

SARGE: (*Turning on the CAPTAIN, the SARGE grabs the CAPTAIN'S shirt.*) Listen, you prick. You may think you're in charge but I run this fuckin' outfit! 'N' wha' I says goes! 'N' if yer don't watch it I'll blow your fuckin' brains out to!

(*The SARGE exits. The CAPTAIN stares at the body of SOLDIER 2 and shakes violently, and finally begins to laugh. Blackout.*)

Scene Two

GABRIEL, who has been left behind, is staring at the dead SOLDIER 2. Time passes.

GABRIEL: Martyr!

(*GABRIEL laughs a sharp, short staccato laugh. Quietly, HENSMAN enters.*)

Didn't know him no never will now – he coils and uncoils elliptical persistence of knowledge purple music with shades of unresolved pain yes coiling to uncoil

(*GABRIEL laughs again.*)

HENSMAN: Was that the Hampshire's that just left? Someone told me it was them.

GABRIEL: He has come and I was found wanting didn't look at me no the pain of fertile glances no warmth in the absence

HENSMAN: I must follow them – if it was them.

GABRIEL: Stay awhile the need to talk to communicate disorientated perspectives I have never felt as lonely as now

HENSMAN: (*Debates this. Finally.*) A while then.

GABRIEL: I have failed him though he forgives always forgives failed everyone fails him and all he does is forgive eons of disappointment

HENSMAN: Forgiveness is pathetic, it perpetuates hatred and contempt. Strength is what we should rely on. It overcomes petty desire, fallibilities – you know war eliminates the feeble. A culling ground of the useless.

GABRIEL: You do not believe that –

HENSMAN: An expert –

GABRIEL: Not your words –

HENSMAN: Knows me for two minutes and –

GABRIEL: I have seen the flicker of love in your eyes shadow puppet of truth buried but alive in twilight hues –

HENSMAN: Love! Who? You?!

GABRIEL: If not me then –

HENSMAN: The audacity of ego!

GABRIEL: How could I love nothing –

HENSMAN: Defiling words with slicing spite –

GABRIEL: There have been moments –

HENSMAN: Wanton aggression –

GABRIEL: Of fragility when eyes sing to each other –

HENSMAN: Malicious vandalism –

GABRIEL: Sighing as trees in the wind –

HENSMAN: Childish abandon –

GABRIEL: In desolate forlorn places –

HENSMAN: Decadent brutality –

GABRIEL: And the patter of love descending as midnight
snow –

HENSMAN: Again! That word!

GABRIEL: As around us barren lasciviousness –

HENSMAN: Mangling sensitivity –

GABRIEL: We sit and stare and heartbeats in time
sorrowfully whisper and it is dawn –

HENSMAN: (*Lashes out and hits GABRIEL.*) Barbarian! You
cannot steal words!

(*GABRIEL gets up and forcefully kisses HENSMAN.
HENSMAN pushes GABRIEL away and hits him. Again
GABRIEL moves forward and forcefully kisses HENSMAN.
HENSMAN pushes GABRIEL away and hits him again.
This time before GABRIEL can kiss HENSMAN,
HENSMAN hits GABRIEL so hard that GABRIEL falls
to the ground.*)

Thief! You play with words as if they are common
currency – you cannot love: it is not your word!

(*GABRIEL regards HENSMAN for the moment. Finally.*)

GABRIEL: In the abandoning willow-o-wisp hope darts this
and that way and gamble and bet I have sacrificed
everything for you

HENSMAN: Holes in the pocket, every step you take
makes you poorer –

GABRIEL: We two misfits and charlatans here we should
not be let us go together –

HENSMAN: (*Grabbing GABRIEL by the lapels and dragging
him nearer.*) I am here for something beyond your
comprehension.

GABRIEL: I will help –

HENSMAN: Nonsense –

GABRIEL: As snow is to silence for us where is the divide?

HENSMAN: It is sin, Gabriel.

GABRIEL: The book has fallen from my grasp the vision
tumbles and all I hear is my stained blood beating for
you…anything…

HENSMAN: Anything?

GABRIEL: The wire pins me the mud sucks me down and annihilation sits grinning you to me is all I have…anything

HENSMAN: (*Regards GABRIEL.*) So I see.

(*HENSMAN hits GABRIEL again and again, and just as GABRIEL can take no more, HENSMAN kisses him quickly, then exits. Time. GABRIEL slumps, exhausted. He spots the dead SOLDIER 2 and laughs his staccato laugh.*)

GABRIEL: Martyr!

(*Blackout.*)

Scene Three

The CAPTAIN enters. He is wide-eyed and when still, trembles. At some point he has fallen into the mud and his uniform is filthy from it. He has lost his gun and hat. Although there is silence, the CAPTAIN reacts as if there is an artillery barrage – imagining the shells exploding around him. He continues this grotesque dance until he falls over. He howls like an animal.

CAPTAIN: Always the s-s-same always the s-s-same as if pain is a charm bracelet w-w-w-wanted to stay oh let me stay (*He laughs, trembles, and ends up howling again.*) now he yes he he k-k-knows does too does indeed like the sky falls in-in-in bang-bang-bang-bang rip it out rip it out (*Trying to get up, the CAPTAIN falls again. This quiets him down.*) are you here p-p-please be here missed you so much just a little cuddley-wuddley to hold you again hold-hold-hold you again oh Sandra the men are so corrupt pigs w-w-wallowing in filth and the cruelness of it it's all bankrupt bankrupt all of it impossible things doing impossible things m-m-my body can only do so m-m-much and your soft skin silk-veneer need to rest n-n-n-need to rest (*The CAPTAIN starts and tries to get up, protecting himself from an imaginary assailant.*) leave m-m-me alone leave alone don't hit me don't-don't-don't please please don't

(*The CAPTAIN collapses gibbering and curls up on the ground. Time. ANGELIQUE enters, carrying two heavy buckets of water. She staggers under the weight, and doesn't get far before stopping. She rubs her hands and wrists. She sings.*)

ANGELIQUE: 'Tis a violent faded sunrise
'N' all the clouds do topple
With shades of jagged blues and reds
They pound the earth with tears
My lover did wake anon
'N' cried in my cold arms
For the drum called out his name
With a deadly beat beat-beat
So please forgive me sister
In the colding white hushed night
I need something to fill me
So let your man put it in again
Let your man put it in again
(*She laughs.*)

CAPTAIN: (*Looking up.*) S-S-S-Sandra?

ANGELIQUE: Often the dead talk
Like glass scrapped over iron
Best ignore the whispers
For as tunes spin in the mind
They never go away

CAPTAIN: No...grinding silence...h-h-help me...

ANGELIQUE: You must not hurt me
Whatever else
Don't hurt me
Like anything else
I bend only so much

CAPTAIN: Just...need r-r-rest

ANGELIQUE: Even so

CAPTAIN: Not good at this...no...not this...anything actually...here for f-f-father...yes his life I lead...the carrying of a father's obsession is terrifying

ANGELIQUE: You may touch
Prod
Maul any part

But not hurt

Understood?

CAPTAIN: (*Gets up slowly.*) You t-t-talk as if…as if prophesising some…as if you want to!

ANGELIQUE: You are not a man

(*During the following, ANGELIQUE obeys the CAPTAIN.*)

CAPTAIN: Christ…just the bloody s-s-same…just the get down now…try and try to ignore the f-f-filth…but all around as raise your skirt…won't go away no n-n-not away…separates us chalk and cheese open your legs…just a little while a little while…

(*The CAPTAIN drops his trousers and lays on top of ANGELIQUE. She remains completely motionless. He rapes her, slowly. During the act, the CAPTAIN tries to put ANGELIQUE's arms around him, but they fall off as dead things. ANGELIQUE stares ahead. The CAPTAIN repeats the name 'Sandra' over and over and finishes very quickly. After a while, he rolls off her. Time.*)

ANGELIQUE: It was good

No hurt

Good

'Twas nothing

(*ANGELIQUE sits up and smoothes out her dress. The CAPTAIN does up his trousers and stands.*)

It was good not to hurt

Such a ridiculous hurt here

Demeans the horror of these fields

That is no laughing matter

This

This is giggles

(*The CAPTAIN regards ANGELIQUE then begins kicking her in a frenzy of violence. ANGELIQUE curls up and tries to defend herself, but the CAPTAIN's blows pound her. He exhausts himself and stops. He stands over her for a while and spots a ring on her finger. He takes it off, puts it on, and staggers off, dodging imaginary shells. Time. ANGELIQUE slowly uncurls, softly crying.*)

ANGELIQUE: Always hurt
Always hurt
Always hurt
(Blackout.)

Scene Four

A terrible scream. BERT is discovered lying prostrate on the ground, in agony. JOHN enters and immediately applies medical aid to BERT.

BERT: Bin 'it – bin 'it! Fuckin' 'ell! Bin fuckin' 'it!

JOHN: Ease up, Bert, ease up –

BERT: Can't feel me legs – fuckin' numb! Fuckin' 'ell, bin 'it!

JOHN: Bert, listen to me. You have got to stop moving! I can't –

BERT: Wha' 'bout fuckin' Dotty? Yer gotta tell 'er son, tell 'er I thinks of 'er all the fuckin' time –

JOHN: *(Produces a syringe.)* Tell her yourself, you're not going any where –

BERT: Wha' the fuck is tha'?
(BERT screams in agony again as JOHN injects him.)

JOHN: Don't be stupid, Bert, it'll help you. Should take effect soon, just hold on, son –

BERT: Am I gonna die, John?

JOHN: I ain't a medic, you know that –

BERT: Yer always were a fuckin' crap liar –

JOHN: Just try and rest –

BERT: Got no legs, mate! Fuck restin'! 'Elp us!

JOHN: *(Slaps BERT hard.)* Now shut up! You fucking hang on, Bert, don't go crazy on me –

BERT: Sum bleedin' 'elp yer is. Christ, wha' a fuckin' mess.
(BERT sighs and seems more comfortable.)

JOHN: Feeling any better? Is the pain receding?

BERT: Don't know – can't feel much now – just a sorta…nothing'…

JOHN: Easy, son, soon have you out of here.

BERT: Dotty will be mad as 'ell – 'You come 'ome, Bert me old son, 'n' don' go playin' at bleedin' heroes,' she says – blimey, I'm dyin' 'n' I ain't even killed no one –

JOHN: You aren't going to die, Bert –

BERT: Didn't even give 'er a child – all she ever wanted – a fuckin' baby – didn't even give 'er one –

JOHN: Time for that –

BERT: 'Ow long we been friends, John? Couple o' years?

JOHN: I guess so –

BERT: Me 'n' Dotty 'ad a 'ell of a fight over yer – she didn't want yer to live with us – fuck me, she even 'it me with a fryin' pan –

JOHN: I didn't know that, Bert.

BERT: Bit emotional, my Dotty – didn't like yer – no, not at all – thought yer was a funny bugger – 'no real man would lock 'imself in a room 'n' paint pots o' flowers' – 'er words.

JOHN: Well, it turned out all right in the end.

BERT: Aye, did tha'… John?…

JOHN: Yes, Bert.

BERT: You look after 'er –

JOHN: Shut up, Bert –

BERT: Nah, I mean… I know wha' 'appened, like…

JOHN: What are you talking about, Bert?

BERT: You 'n' 'er –

JOHN: Look, son, there was no 'me and her'. It's the drug talking. You just rest a while.

BERT: Well, yer sees, John… I don't wanna call yer a liar, but it 'as to be said, yer is now… I 'eard yer… 'n'… I saw yer…just after we buried me old ma…you remember…don't yer?

(*Time. BERT sighs heavily and JOHN regards him with shame, unable to say anything at all.*)

Always emotional – guess she fell in love with yer, eh? Don't matter though – nah, 'ow could it? Me 'n' yer is mates – shared everythin' we have – why not share old Dotty, eh? She don't mind – especially if she loves yer – maybe she loves us both – nah, nuthin' to worry 'bout – nuthin' at all…

JOHN: Bert, I...

BERT: Fuck me, John, first time yer ever lost for words...
(*BERT laughs but the laugh turns into an agonizing cough.
He wheezes and finally settles down.*)
Fancy dyin' in a fuckin' field – me old ma used to say I'd
die in the fuckin' gutter 'cause I drank so much – is it
getting dark, John?

JOHN: (*Looks up. The lighting hasn't changed.*) Yes, Bert,
getting on for night.

BERT: People always die at night, don't they – well, those
who ain't blown to bits out 'ere...do yer love 'e?

JOHN: Bert...no...

BERT: Gonna be tough on 'er – don't expect the pension's
gonna be much use –

JOHN: I could...could send her money...or...

BERT: To proud for tha' – likely to tell yer to fuck off...if
yer ain't gonna stay with tha' is...

JOHN: You...you don't...hate me...do you, Bert?

BERT: Nah, course not – me 'n' yer we've been thru 'ell 'n'
back, ain't we? Don't need to forgive mates –

JOHN: But I want your forgiveness, Bert.

BERT: Draw me.

JOHN: What?

BERT: I knows yer draws all 'em others... I want yer to
draw me – sumthin' for 'er to remember me by –

JOHN: How? When? Have you a photo?

BERT: Nah, I meant...now...draw me like this...

JOHN: I – I – I –

BERT: It's getting' dark, mate...very dark... 'n' I can feel it
comin' closer –

JOHN: What is?

BERT: Tha' bloke who's always in the corner of yer
eye...yer never can catch a glimpse of 'im...very crafty –

JOHN: Can you see him now, Bert?

BERT: Aye...big bugger – tha's wha' yer want, ain't it?
Capture 'im in my eyes...
(*Time.*)

JOHN: Yes –

BERT: Then...draw me...

> (*JOHN takes out his pencil and pad and begins to draw the dying BERT. Time. JOHN stops often and simply looks at BERT. Finally, JOHN gives up. He throws down his pencil and rips up his pad. BERT dies, almost unnoticed. JOHN stares at BERT for a while, then lowers his head. One sob escapes him. Without raising his head, JOHN holds BERT's hand. But JOHN never cries.*
> *Blackout.*)

Scene Five

ANGELIQUE is discovered in the arms of DIDIER. He rocks her gently and sobs. ANGELIQUE lies still.

ANGELIQUE: Always hurt

> Always hurt
>
> Always hurt

DIDIER: Darling... I am so sorry...sorry sorry sorry

ANGELIQUE: (*No more than whispering.*)

> They climbed the mountain high
>
> And shed no tears to hear
>
> The wind did moan and tumble around
>
> For she is gone that once stood proud

DIDIER: Hush-hush my darling, rest, someone comes to help, hush-hush now –

ANGELIQUE: Father

> Sight falls from my eyes
>
> And in the remembered fracturing
>
> Colours already fading
>
> And grey
>
> Grey
>
> Grey
>
> (*JESUS enters. DIDIER sees him and shakes his head.*)

DIDIER: I am afraid...

JESUS: Desecration upon desecration

> What else tainted?
>
> What stained?
>
> Didier she has half left this world already

DIDIER: (*Howls with pain.*) I will not let go never let go
never
(*DIDIER sobs.*)
ANGELIQUE: Father
I can taste the colours of your despair
Tis bitter almonds
And cold
Cry me colourful love
DIDIER: And safe and warm I will hold you and
everywhere flowers explode and butterflies dance for you
JESUS: Hanging on the wire
We wait to fall
Our eyes pinned eternally open
Waiting
Let me help her, Didier
DIDIER: (*Eyes JESUS suspiciously.*) How? How?
JESUS: She needs to pass –
DIDIER: No!
(*DIDIER howls again.*)
ANGELIQUE: Heavy
Weighting down
Sinking
Forgive them
You must
DIDIER: Never never never they will answer they will
JESUS: Let her pass, Didier
(*DIDIER finally nods, still crying and rocking ANGELIQUE.*
She hums faintly, but otherwise is still. JESUS kneels down
besides her and puts his hand on her forehead.)
Such pain searing souring pain how he hurt me how he
hurt me knew he would yes tasted it colours jaded slicing
tasted the grief anger of suns exploding sinking down
down down dragged under hurting yes hurting speak to
me in colours of joy and touch me not hurt not hurt
No more
(*ANGELIQUE dies. DIDIER howls in anguish. JESUS*
stands and moves away.)

DIDIER: I will not forgive them will not forgive them will
not
JESUS: It makes little difference
DIDIER: You – you want me to – that's what you're about
forgiveness – forgiveness isn't a bauble to lightly toss
away
JESUS: Your grief won't stop the world turning
DIDIER: The ego of the dead
(*DIDIER gets up.*)
They didn't punish you enough
JESUS: Hit me
(*DIDIER is confused, but at JESUS' silent prompting,
DIDER hits JESUS.*)
Again
(*DIDIER does so.*)
No – harder
(*DIDIER hits JESUS and knocks him off his feet.*)
Again
(*DIDIER launches himself at JESUS and tries to strangle
him. The two are locked in a grotesque embrace, but JESUS
doesn't attempt to stop DIDIER. Finally, exhausted, DIDIER
lets go and staggers back, panting.*)
Until you can stamp me out of your heart, your anger is
useless – bury your dead
(*JESUS exits. DIDIER slumps down besides ANGELIQUE
and sobs.
Blackout.*)

Scene Six

*JESUS sits contemplating the battlefield. GABRIEL enters and
watches JESUS for a while.*

JESUS: In the silence...such colours...these colours hidden
in the maelstrom awake with a fragility...as if noise wilts
them...jewels scattered amongst the slaughterhouse...like
hell itself –
GABRIEL: Hell? You know hell?
JESUS: I know its subtle nuances, yes.

GABRIEL: You make it sound like an attractive place.

JESUS: There is no place that is completely devoid of God's love...except some hearts...

GABRIEL: You ignored me –

JESUS: The ignorer ignoring the ignorant –

GABRIEL: **If your gonna be sarcastic** –

JESUS: Gabriel, even your language has lost the divine.

GABRIEL: I... I know.

JESUS: That uniform – you have joined an army?

GABRIEL: No, they... I couldn't wear white –

JESUS: Why?

GABRIEL: It became...stained...

JESUS: Ah...

GABRIEL: You must know what happened?

JESUS: Yes, only I don't know why.

GABRIEL: It's all so overwhelming – the noise and clamour – even the earth heaves and shakes – the incineration of beauty – men – good innocent men – dying for obscure reasons – how they bellow and holler – the frenzied hacking and ripping – and each side professing god's love – **a procession of calamity** – overwhelming – I was not prepared...

JESUS: Not the reason –

GABRIEL: I was scared –

JESUS: Not the reason –

GABRIEL: In the quickening reptilian speed –

JESUS: **Not the reason** –

GABRIEL: **What do you want me to say?** Love – another kind of love – what's wrong with love?

JESUS: It is not love, Gabriel –

GABRIEL: **How dare you say that** –

JESUS: You free fall in every direction –

GABRIEL: Shut up!

JESUS: Where is the purchase? The hold –

(*GABRIEL grabs JESUS and stands face to face with him.*)

GABRIEL: **Do not condemn me** –

JESUS: You will not be snagged, no wire is strong enough –

GABRIEL: **Do not abandon me, you fuck** –

(*Somehow GABRIEL is thrown back across the stage and lands in a heap, panting. JESUS regards him, then explodes in fury.*)

JESUS: There lies the intelligent fool, prostrate in controlled fury, feeling brave cowardice, oh, you people, with the deceits and half-lies and **you do not blame yourselves**, everywhere responsibility clangs to the ground, loose change that everyone ignores, **come here**! (*GABRIEL gets up and begins to walk toward JESUS.*) Living the lives you do not want to live, saying the things you do not want to say, and the weight of breathing, heavy-heavy, the effort, to stay above, to rise free, to soar above the cacophony, **sloth pumps through your veins**

(*JESUS grabs GABRIEL and before GABRIEL can stop him, unzips GABRIEL's trousers and thrusts his hand in.*) **Is this your love?**

(*JESUS begins to masturbate GABRIEL, who now, is struggling to break free.*) You whine about love and fail to see it slip through your fingers **that any better?** You reject the eternal for a transience of seconds my how you pursue it the effort you spend **exhaust yourself for a dribble of juice** moan for me Gabriel grind and thrust yourself **abandon yourself for me**

(*GABRIEL finally breaks free, but in doing so, falls to the ground. JESUS stands over him and jams his foot beneath GABRIEL'S throat.*) Flee, Gabriel, for you have sunk, sucked down into the mud, your soul ripped and torn, hanging on the wire, with the desolation of the void around you, flee, for the night comes without stars, the moon blood-red, and the folding, crushing weight is guilt unsustained and it will trample you like an insect –

(*JESUS releases GABRIEL and exits. GABRIEL remains on the floor, choking and crying at the same time. Blackout.*)

Scene Seven

The SARGE enters closely followed by the CAPTAIN, who is still as dishevelled as before, and every now and then ducks unseen explosions.

CAPTAIN: W-w-we must speak –

SARGE: Not now – gotta get the men ready –

CAPTAIN: That's an o-o-order, sergeant –

SARGE: Shut up, yer foolish fuck –

CAPTAIN: I shall enforce this, you know.

(*The SARGE stops and looks at the CAPTAIN.*)

SARGE: Right then, wha' do yer want?

CAPTAIN: T-t-that's better, sergeant.

(*Time.*)

SARGE: Well?

CAPTAIN: A d-d-delicate matter –

SARGE: For fuck sake's, spit it out –

CAPTAIN: I n-n-need you to do something for me –

SARGE: Tha'd be novel –

CAPTAIN: Look here, Sergeant, h-h-how much do you earn?

SARGE: Wha'?

CAPTAIN: Pay – you know –

SARGE: Fuck all, really –

CAPTAIN: Precisely!

SARGE: So?

CAPTAIN: How would you like to earn…fifty pounds?

(*The CAPTAIN produces a wad of money. The SARGE stares at it and the CAPTAIN.*)

SARGE: A lotta money, tha' is… (*Laughs.*) Christ, sir, wha' the fuck do yer: want me to do?

CAPTAIN: I-I-I-I w-w-want…shoot me!

(*Time.*)

Please I…please, just do it… I-I-I mean…

(*Time.*)

Please…please…

(*Time.*)

C-c-can't do this any m-m-more…got to go home…

SARGE: Where d'want it?

CAPTAIN: (*Trembles and shakes.*) Hadn't thought –

SARGE: The knee's always best – if yer can't fuckin' walk, yer can't fuckin' fight, can yer?

CAPTAIN: Right...t-t-the knee...how do you want –

(*Without warning, the SARGE pulls out a revolver and shoots the CAPTAIN twice in the knee. The CAPTAIN falls to the ground in screaming agony. He rolls and twitches. The SARGE approaches him, putting away the revolver.*)

SARGE: Always wanted to do tha'. Sit still, you shit.

(*Ignoring the CAPTAIN's agony, the SARGE takes the money from the CAPTAIN. Satisfied, the SARGE puts away the money and takes out a dagger.*)

Gotta do this right – if you've been shot in the knee, yer musta been standin' up – in battle, maybe – if tha's true, then yer would've 'ad more injuries – cut on the wire, like –

(*The SARGE casually cuts the CAPTAIN on the face. The CAPTAIN howls.*)

Maybe a bleedin' bayonet wound –

(*The SARGE stabs the CAPTAIN, who is bleeding badly now.*)

Even sum fisty-cuffs –

(*The SARGE hits the CAPTAIN repeatedly until the CAPTAIN passes out. Exhausted, the SARGE stands back to admire his work.*)

Cunt!

(*BRAD enters.*)

BRAD: Jesus! Is that the captain?

SARGE: Wha' do yer want, lumberjack?

BRAD: What the fuck happened to him?

SARGE: 'E fell!

BRAD: What? But there's been no attack – ...what happened here, you bastard?

SARGE: Listen, yer piece of fuck, I found 'im 'ere, didn't I?

BRAD: Let me see him –

(*BRAD tries to get past the SARGE to examine the CAPTAIN, but at that moment the SARGE lunges at BRAD trying to stab him. BRAD reacts quickly and deflects the attack and manages to hit the SARGE with his rifle butt. The SARGE is stunned but manages to try another stab. BRAD easily moves out of the way and hits the SARGE again, this time on his head. The SARGE falls to his knees, the dagger falling from his hand. BRAD steps forward and hits the SARGE again on the head. The SARGE collapses to the ground and is still. BRAD stands over the SARGE and rises his rifle to strike again. He holds it suspended above the SARGE's head, but cannot bring it down. Instead he stumbles away howling with rage. Time. BRAD realises the position he is in, and panics. He checks the CAPTAIN then the SARGE and after a second or two of thought, bolts from the stage. Time. The SARGE recovers somewhat, but he does not move. Instead, he talks out loud.*)

SARGE: Stumblin' shame yes darlin' yes darlin' who won the three thirty man-o-war man-o-war miss yer 'n' yer smiling' eyes twenty guineas 'n' me stake back yes lads on me tha' water mind tha' water shame on yer shame t'was Kempton Park just a couple aye 'n' the chasers didn't mean it just not looking' 'n' the water twenty guineas little darlin' man-o-war tha's me miss yer miss yer shame on yer shame black water just a second ice-black water not my fault believe me believe me little darlin' little darlin'

(HENSMAN and GABRIEL enter. GABRIEL is clearly pestering HENSMAN who has seen the sight of the unconscious CAPTAIN and the delirious SARGE.)

GABRIEL: It's over! Talked it through – over!

HENSMAN: Shut up!

GABRIEL: We can leave now – you and I – leave –

HENSMAN: God in heaven, look at this –

GABRIEL: Anywhere – we can go anywhere – nothing can stop us –

HENSMAN: (*Examining the CAPTAIN.*) This one's still alive – get help – now!

GABRIEL: This is no longer our concern –

HENSMAN: (*Moving over to the SARGE.*) Just go and...

GABRIEL: What is it?

HENSMAN: Justice…

GABRIEL: Pardon? Are you listening to –

HENSMAN: (*Emotionless.*) Hold both of his arms –

GABRIEL: What?

HENSMAN: Lift his arms behind his head – hold them there –

GABRIEL: Why?

HENSMAN: Do it!

> (*GABRIEL kneels behind the head of the SARGE and brings both his arms up behind them. HENSMAN straddles the SARGE's stomach. GABRIEL is just about to say something, when HENSMAN pulls out a dagger and rips the SARGE's stomach open, plunging the knife deeper and deeper. GABRIEL screams in horror and lets go of the SARGE's arms. The SARGE quickly dies. GABRIEL sits whimpering. HENSMAN leaves the knife in and spits on the SARGE's face.*)

That's for Margaret, you utter cunt!

> (*HENSMAN slumps back, knife in hand. GABRIEL sits staring, still whimpering. HENSMAN takes off his helmet and shakes down his/her long hair. She throws away the helmet and begins to unbuckle her webbing. GABRIEL stirs.*)

Two years been following his trail – two years. Seems like my whole life – one camp to another – one battle to another – still he lived – luck of the devil – the devil – dead now – yes – stuck a fucking pin in his guts – fat guts – dead cunt

GABRIEL: I… I…don't…

HENSMAN: Was me – killed our little one – Margaret – Margaret…

> (*HENSMAN cries.*)

Two years – black water – ice-black water…

GABRIEL: I helped you…kill…

HENSMAN: Floating like a lily she was…drifting and turning…looked like she was flying…an angel flying…

GABRIEL: This has…been a sign…the two of us…complicit…

HENSMAN: It is over now…no more now…

GABRIEL: I will follow you – now and forever – the two of us –

(*HENSMAN looks up at GABRIEL.*)

HENSMAN: Come here…

(*GABRIEL gets up and goes to HENSMAN.*)

No more –

(*HENSMAN stabs GABRIEL in his good eye. GABRIEL collapses clutching at his eye and sobbing.*)

No more…

(*HENSMAN slowly exits. GABRIEL has fallen now and passes out with the pain. Time. JESUS enters and ignores the scene around him. Instead, he sits and contemplates. Finally, the CAPTAIN comes round, and with difficulty, sits up.*)

CAPTAIN: Some attack – out of the blue – hundreds of the screaming Hun – good fight – yes – good fight…well, that's the story – who cares – a medal – or two – got them – open doors though – way of the world – now I'm hurt – that is, really hurt – suffered – yes – suffered – we all have but for me – not my bag – all this – no – not this – don't know why I'm here – or any of us for that matter – still – business – helps business – all this – be there soon – soon – very soon – get picked up – hospital – sympathy – another medal – that's why uniform is so wide – to hold all those medals – can't wait, frankly – can't wait – it'll be good to have dinner in Mayfair again – see the boys – well, some dead, of course – but some still there – you know, this war is like a business plan – wiping the slate clean – yes – start again – older lot – got it wrong – so wrong – all that honour and duty – god sakes – you can buy that anytime you want to – money – power – bed mates, you know – then we'll see – they scorn us, you know – this scum – British – can't be – most of them – no backbone – no spirit – the British aren't about fighting up to their balls in this filth – no, sir – no indeed – we're above that – untainted – rule the world through subtlety – influence – discretion – back to money – the world respects money – and background – not like those Yanks – peasants the lot of them – vulgar

money – money – yes – money – going to make heaps
and heaps – making bullets – you got some spare cash –
could strike a deal – no – maybe not – anyway, don't
want to share – why should I – making bullets – sell
them to both sides – perpetuate the war – need more
bullets – make more money – etc, etc – anyone who
wants them – anyone – that's the trick – you a priest –
vicar – you and your lot – defunct – old time – I've seen
the way you lot ingratiate yourselves – bowing and
scraping – clinging on to the tails of power – money –
we'll buy you – and your god – god's a commodity –
buy and sell him – to us, the Hun, Christ, even the
foreigners will buy that one – buy god – yes – why not –
he'd admire industry – spirit – a new world order –
upheaval – a new god – a new man – we dictate the
future – man – yes – no gods – all that fire and
brimstone – money will buy that – we'll build weapons
that will blow god from his high seat – make him work
for a change – and this scum – feed them to the pigs –
give them enough to work a bit harder – making us
richer – yes – money – sex-money – war-
money – love-money – hate-money – god-money – yes –
god-money –
(*JESUS has been impassive, but now he explodes into anger.
The lights blind with white intensity, and the theatre shakes
with rumbles.*)

JESUS: Kneel, little man before thy eternity in your
arrogance, mock your own foolishness, you dabble in
powers beyond your comprehension, so this is man, his
achievements and ambitions pollute the skies, poison the
soil, and now he thinks himself god, down snake, down,
for I am the keeper of the dead, rise, rise captured souls
(*THE DEAD, who litter the stage, begin to slowly rise up,
animated corpses. The CAPTAIN is terrified beyond words
and scrabbles to get away.*)
The sky falls down burning white-red, incinerating words
and souls, the ground heaves and erupts, and skin melts,
eyes burst, blood rains down swallowing the drowning,

and bones snap and crack, the drums of annihilation,
behold the wailing of the burnt
(*A guttural lament is heard. The CAPTAIN is being hemmed
in by THE DEAD.*)
Behold the Man-God
(*The CAPTAIN, in his terror, stumbles into some wire and is
caught by it. JESUS advances closer to him.*)
Wrap him with his own conceits
(*The CAPTAIN tries to struggle but only succeeds in becoming
more tangled and snagged in the wire.*)
Crush crush and crush the insect Man-God
(*THE DEAD force the CAPTAIN's arms back and completely
pin him on the wire. JESUS stands before the CAPTAIN,
and has a large stake, or fencing post, in his hands.*)
Let Man-God wallow in this world – let this world be an
abandoned place – let this world be Man-God's world
(*JESUS pins the CAPTAIN with the stake and pushes it
slowly through the CAPTAIN's chest. Screams, wailing, noise,
and lights.*)
So it begins!
(*The CAPTAIN dies in great agony. THE DEAD howl and
depart. The theatre shakes. The lights blind. Silence. Time.
JESUS stands before the dead CAPTAIN. BRAD, JOHN,
and DIDIER, enter.*)
BRAD: Mother of Christ!
(*DIDIER rushes up to the CAPTAIN and tries to attend to
him. JOHN has found the SARGE. BRAD is stunned.*)
What happened?
JESUS: The beginning
BRAD: Of what?
JESUS: Something stronger
BRAD: What the fuck –
(*DIDIER finds ANGELIQUE's ring on the CAPTAIN's
finger. He pulls it off.*)
DIDIER: Her ring...
JESUS: Yes, and forgiveness?
DIDIER: None.
BRAD: Did you do this? Look at Gabriel!

JOHN: (*Producing a scrap of paper and a pen, he begins to draw the SARGE.*) The butchery – the ripped skin – the torn organs – life evaporating red

JESUS: I go now

BRAD: You bastard – you can't leave –

JOHN: Harlequin mutilation – life as decayed slime –

BRAD: You can't fucking go –

(*JESUS and DIDIER exit to BRAD's remonstrations. GABRIEL awakes and crawls, bumping into the CAPTAIN's leg. GABRIEL feels the body and discovers it position and the fact that it is dead.*)

GABRIEL: Dead...dead again...dead...

BRAD: Come back here, you bastard – you can't just leave – you can't just leave –

(*JOHN draws. GABRIEL hums a lament. BRAD slumps to the ground, dazed. Somewhere, the shelling starts again.*)

The End

BEREZINA

Characters

NAPOLEON

NEY

BERNADETTE

BERNADETTE's FATHER

GABRIELLE

ARNOUX

OUDINOT

EUGENIE

EUGENIE's FATHER

PILS

TORZHOK

LE TELLIER

FRENCH OFFICERS

FRENCH SOLDIERS

RUSSIAN SOLDIERS

THE DEAD

Berezina was first performed by Concussion Productions at the White Bear Theatre, London, on Tuesday 11 April 2005, with the following cast confirmed at the time of going to press:

BERNADETTE, Cat Edgecombe

GABRIELLE, Lucy Fredrick

SOLDIER 3, Nick Gale

EUGENIE, Jo Hammett

NEY, Mark Healy

SOLDIER 1, Peter Henderson

PILS, Joe Hunt

SOLDIER 2, Sean McAleese

TORZHOK, Paul Murthwaite

NAPOLEON, James O'Donnell

SARGE, Tom Woodman

Directed by Vincent Adams

ACT ONE

Scene One

The stage is dark. The lights rise, on a dancing couple. OUDINOT and EUGENIE dance to waltz music. The music is far-away, and distorted, echoing as if in a dream. The couple dance very slowly and not in time to the music. They dance close together. OUDINOT moves away from EUGENIE, as if going to spin her around. She smiles, happy and content. However, OUDINOT reacts as if he is shot. His body arches up, and pain spreads across his face. EUGENIE, horrified is unable to move, but tries to reach out to OUDINOT. OUDINOT is hit again, and falls backwards in slow-motion. The lights have been rising constantly since OUDINOT first got hit, and by now they have become bright white, intense, dazzling on the white set. The glare is disorientating, disturbing. The music jars, skips, and becomes discordant. In this overwhelming state THE DEAD enter, black smudges against the fierceness. THE DEAD already chant/whisper lines from the play – those yet to come and those just about to be said. This is their motif, the tilted time that envelops them. Their movements are jagged, imprecise, blurred, and yet somehow organic. Their voices echo around the theatre, and they bring cold to the white-hot intensity. OUDINOT falls back into their arms and they shift him upwards through the space. As they do so, they begin THE FIRST PROLOGUE OF THE DEAD.

THE DEAD: The swirling pale
    Swiftingly float-float
    As butterflies a-delicate
    And hover and quiver
    The whispering death
    Float-float
    Sleep creeping and tumbling
    Down-down float-float
    Nothing comes quick enough
    Making black music
    Marks against the purity

Float-float
Come they heaving and
Grunting float-float
With unnatural natures
Raising the deep
Drowning the cold stars
Float-float
Ego of the
Unalive float-float
Innocence buried blue
Melting hearts
Waiting for the burning rain
Float-float
Float-float

(*THE DEAD, taking OUDINOT with them, scuttle out of the lights, which dim to a more acceptable level. EUGENIE holds out her hands to nothing, and she too, slowly fades from the scene. THE DEAD shuffle and dart around the stage, unseen, but present. Occasional echoes and whispers are heard. NEY enters. Dishevelled, tired, and wrapped against the cold, he hardly looks like a Marshal of France. He stares around him, trying to catch a glimpse of THE DEAD. He seems on the verge of violence.*)

NEY: As if...**if I catch you buggers**... I mean an enemy that refuses to show itself...a secret enemy...watching the cupboard rattle...**s'not fuckin' funny**...ten days...ten days slippin' 'n' slidin' in this white shit...keepin' hold of...graspin' the... 'n' behind...invisible sniggers...**there will come a time when**... I will grind you until the colours come out...

NAPOLEON: (*Entering.*) Moaning again, Ney?

NEY: (*Surprised.*) My Lord –

NAPOLEON: For pisses sake, Ney, can't you once be positive, I mean...**a little bit of positivity**...hardly asking for the stars...am I?

NEY: No –

NAPOLEON: A smile –

NEY: Look here –

NAPOLEON: Grin –

NEY: I said –

NAPOLEON: Grimace –

NEY: Don't take –

NAPOLEON: Frown –

NEY: Take the piss –

NAPOLEON: **Do it!**

> (*NEY struggles, but eventually produces a lop-sided and forced grin. Silence floats around a while.*)
> That...wasn't worth the energy. What are you doing out here?

NEY: Just...nothing...

NAPOLEON: Ney, my army is like an exquisite ice sculpture, yet drip by drip it dissipates, nothing can ever put it back again, each step, steps through the river, swelling, rising river, we plunge on, beat-beat-beat, each step... I need men of stone, Ney...stone-men.

NEY: Am –

NAPOLEON: Then –

NEY: Eight years –

NAPOLEON: Staring into –

NEY: Seventeen before that –

NAPOLEON: Into the mist –

NEY: For you –

NAPOLEON: Impenetrable mist –

NEY: To fuck with –

NAPOLEON: Probing unseen depths –

NEY: Like a fuckin' dog –

NAPOLEON: Going soft –

NEY: Fuck you –

NAPOLEON: **Soft as shit** –

NEY: **Hear them!**...that's all...hear them...

NAPOLEON: Oh...them!

NEY: You have heard them?

NAPOLEON: (*Looking around.*) They have never left me...never ever.

NEY: What? I...you mean...an enemy?

NAPOLEON: (*Dismissing it.*) Give me a report of the rearguard –

NEY: Tell me –

NAPOLEON: Boring –

NEY: Tell me –

NAPOLEON: **Boring** –

NEY: **What the fuck are they?**

(*NAPOLEON exits. NEY continues to stare out into the theatre, trying to catch a glimpse of THE DEAD. Finally, fear overcomes him, and NEY exits to the sound of footfalls and echoes and whispers.*)

Scene Two

A battle. A huge explosion. We hear men shout and scream. Confusion and movement. TWO SOLDIERS and PILS enter, carrying the wounded figure of MARSHAL OUDINOT. They lay him down gingerly.

PILS: Quickly – you! Inform His Majesty – Marshal Oudinot is hit! You! Find Marshal Ney – he must assume command! Go!

(*The TWO SOLDIERS exit quickly.*)

OUDINOT: (*Wheezing and breathing very hard.*) Pils... Pils...

PILS: Shut up! Bullet in the lungs! Don't move, man!

OUDINOT: Dying –

PILS: An expert! Pah! Lie still! Damn this blood – **where is the hole?**

(*PILS probes OUDINOT's body trying to find the bullet hole. OUDINOT squirms in agony.*)

OUDINOT: What...of Eugenie?

PILS: What of her? My sister is probably, even as we speak, buying more ridiculous dresses – you know the type – neckline too low, skirt too fancy, and frills! Frills everywhere! When we get back, you should tell my sister that frills went out with the Bourbons!

OUDINOT: Look...after...her –

PILS: God sakes! Be quiet! How many wounds have you had? Eh? Thirty two? Three? This – this mere scratch, why, I've seen worse when you shave! Now be quiet!

OUDINOT: Must...say...things...

PILS: Talk! Talk! Like a damn woman! You and my sister make a perfect pair! Try fucking more! Ah-ha!
(*PILS suddenly digs deeper and harder, probing right into OUDINOT's body. Screams from OUDINOT.*)
I have it! Be still you pig-dog! **Still!**
(*More thrashing about and screaming. PILS refuses to be put off, and takes a bayonet out which he uses to dig deeper.*)
I feel it! I have it! Steady! Steady! Yes!
(*PILS pulls a small metal object out of OUDINOT's side. PILS examines it, oblivious to OUDINOT's pain.*)
A pissing button! Piss and damn! A fucking button! Must have been blown into you by the bullet! Shit! Sit still, we go again!

OUDINOT: (*Gasping in pain.*) In a minute...please...a minute...

PILS: Fine! A minute to get your breath back! Where is that damn doctor? Brandy?

OUDINOT: (*He drinks. Settling, but still breathing hard.*) You...my brother-in-law –

PILS: Well, your memory is fine!

OUDINOT: Things...you should know...a right –

PILS: **I have no rights!** Not connected enough!

OUDINOT: My confession –

PILS: Pah! Church! Pah! Last time I was in a church – trying to fuck a novice nun by the font – do you know what they wear under that black?

OUDINOT: I... I...have...hurt Eugenie...
(*A silence where PILS regards OUDINOT. At last.*)

PILS: I look for the bullet again –

OUDINOT: Listen! (*Pain.*) I had...a mistress –

PILS: Pah! Most men do –

OUDINOT: Hurt...best part of me... Eugenie...

PILS: Hurt?...

OUDINOT: Our first meeting...stumbling into a
dream...her eyes...how they sang...rarest
music...heartbeats in time...echoes that haunt me...

PILS: But you still fucked someone else! So it goes! This
bullet, now –

OUDINOT: Worse...worse...hammer to a rose...

PILS: (*Uneasy.*) Maybe...maybe we don't talk anymore –

OUDINOT: Drunk...always drunk...blot out the
sun...easier drunk...tainting the pure –

PILS: Oudinot, there is no time for this –

OUDINOT: And insisted...insisted –

PILS: What?

OUDINOT: Her face...twisted agony...dulling the voice of
her eyes –

PILS: **What did you do?**

OUDINOT: Rage drifted down upon me...stifling
breath...red breath...and hate... **I wished to rip her
beating heart out and shove it down her throat** –

PILS: She's only a girl, man!

OUDINOT: (*Raising up in his panic.*) Couldn't stop couldn't
stop her heavily pregnant form and the others leering
and smirking and she she knew I had to had to **force it
out of her** the lies and half-truths and deceits **what is
more addictive than a glimpse** and she stood swearing
innocence and fury and barbarity and I hit her **bang
bang** and down-down she went and I raged and raged
and ... she ... bled ... and ...

PILS: My nephew lost ...

OUDINOT: Even the bleeding did not convince me red lies
all of it red lies –

PILS: (*Suddenly thrusting the bayonet into OUDINOT's side
violently.*) I will find that bullet! **I will!** (*OUDINOT is
delirious with pain.*) Fucking bullet! Fucking bullet!

OUDINOT: (*Mixed with screams.*) Do it – do it – do it – to
me –

PILS: (*Stopping.*) What? What, you stupid fuck!

OUDINOT: (*Almost unconscious.*) In the shifting...heaving...
twilight...sorry is pathetic...whisper in the gale...
absolution...absolution...

PILS: Fucking absolution? **Fucking absolution?**
  (*In his fury, PILS stabs OUDINOT slowly, however, PILS begins to cry. He stops, overcome. He throws away the bayonet and sobs on OUDINOT's inert body. A SOLDIER and the DOCTOR enter.*)
SOLDIER: Look! Here they are! The servant and his master!
DOCTOR: My God, what a sight! Overcome by grief! (*To PILS.*) Don't worry, good fellow, we shall save the honest Marshal. **We shall save him!** (*To the SOLDIER.*) Help me, man! (*PILS collapses sobbing and heaving.*) You'll get a medal for this! And the story about how we found you shall ring from the rooftops of Paris. We shall save him! **We shall save him!**

Scene Three

A garden in Wilna. A scream off stage. EUGENIE enters hysterical with fear. She is quickly followed by her FATHER and LE TELLIER. The latter appears exhausted, dirty, and completely frozen. His clothes, once an elaborate military uniform, are rags and covered in bits of clothing stolen from other men. His hands are both bandaged.

EUGENIE's FATHER: Oh, God pity us!
LE TELLIER: Calm yourself, he is alive, he is coming, but…he has received…he is wounded again…a little…here…
  (*LE TELLIER gives EUGENIE a dirty, blood-stained letter. EUGENIE tries to read it, but fails.*)
  Here…let me… 'My dearest Eugenie, do not try to worry when I tell you that I have received a slight wound. Although not serious, it is in my side, and as a result, I have been ordered home. I set out tomorrow and shall be by your side shortly. My love, my own love. Oudinot.'
EUGENIE's FATHER: You see! It is just another wound to show the children!
LE TELLIER: A veritable scratch, little more –
EUGENIE: My loss…here we go again –

EUGENIE's FATHER: My dear! You mustn't allow your
   imagination –

LE TELLIER: Three days – five at the outside – he will be
   here –

EUGENIE: I knew it! I will go to him –

EUGENIE's FATHER: Nonsense!

LE TELLIER: As to that, your husband foresaw your
   project, and he has so rigorously prescribed my line of
   conduct that I will not let you go even if I have to lock
   you up to prevent you.

EUGENIE's FATHER: I see! Even when hundreds of miles
   away he threatens –

LE TELLIER: My lord?

EUGENIE's FATHER: Nothing! Daughter, dear, we have
   been talking only recently, yes? We were coming to a
   decision –

EUGENIE: These shivers...inside – **I had seen this!**

LE TELLIER: May I ask what 'decisions'? My instructions
   were quite clear –

EUGENIE's FATHER: Yes, I bet! This concerns you not,
   Le Tellier.

LE TELLIER: I do not think that is for you to say –

EUGENIE's FATHER: (*Ignoring LE TELLIER.*) Darling, we
   must leave –

LE TELLIER: My orders –

EUGENIE's FATHER: Go back to France –

LE TELLIER: You will stay –

EUGENIE's FATHER: His behaviour will not be
   tolerated –

LE TELLIER: I will enforce this –

EUGENIE's FATHER: **This is not the army, son!**

EUGENIE: The army? What of the Emperor?

EUGENIE's FATHER: Eugenie, please –

EUGENIE: I dreamt...such things –

LE TELLIER: The Emperor! It is his victims that we have
   to think of. His vast, mad enterprise, his boundless
   ambitions, his unequalled selfishness have cost us four
   hundred thousand men...you ask me for news of the

army, Madame: it no longer exists...look at me: I am one of the strongest, one of the best clad of those who, in small numbers and by a miracle, have escaped that immense disaster!

EUGENIE's FATHER: So, it has come to this – more reason to leave!

EUGENIE: I saw...smiling blue crushed –

EUGENIE's FATHER: Enough of your morbid auguries! We leave for France –

LE TELLIER: Again I warn you –

EUGENIE's FATHER: You try my patience, young man –

EUGENIE: If the chaos descends, will not the journey be a greater risk for my husband than for me?

LE TELLIER: No, because he has an escort which you would be without. I repeat, the Marshal's life and journey are safe.

EUGENIE: I see...he foretold that snow speaks silently... I knew it...knew it and heard it...

(*Distantly the waltz music from scene one begins to play – only EUGENIE notices it. She seems transfixed, and ignores the two men.*)

EUGENIE's FATHER: Him! Him! Why always him? Let us talk about what we want –

LE TELLIER: This is not possible –

EUGENIE's FATHER: Eugenie, his behaviour – I mean – even now – **he will do it again if you let him!**

LE TELLIER: I can see now why the Marshal warned me of you –

EUGENIE's FATHER: Really! So when he can't throw his weight around, he sends a lackey –

LE TELLIER: Conceited and overbearing –

EUGENIE's FATHER: Me! What about him?

LE TELLIER: Spreading lies and accusations where none exist –

EUGENIE's FATHER: The colour of bruises is hardly an accusation –

LE TELLIER: 'If you have to, Le Tellier, slap the bastard until he sees sense –'

EUGENIE's FATHER: A slap, eh? His favourite calling
    card –
LE TELLIER: Monsieur, if I have to, I will use force –
EUGENIE's FATHER: Beware of who you speak to –
LE TELLIER: I know well enough –
EUGENIE's FATHER: Raise a finger and my men will cut
    you down where you stand –
LE TELLIER: Give me the excuse to run you through like
    a pig –
EUGENIE's FATHER: Ha! You hear this, Eugenie?
    Nothing changes!
    (*EUGENIE's FATHER turns to EUGENIE, but she is
    long gone, having slipped out while the two men argued.*)
    Where... Eugenie...did you see her go?
LE TELLIER: No... I...
EUGENIE's FATHER: Eugenie! Eugenie!
LE TELLIER: Look! A rider! It is her!
EUGENIE's FATHER: Eugenie! Wait! Wait!
    (*Both men rush off stage.*)

Scene Four

*The road. White frozen. THE DEAD litter the landscape, some half
buried by the snow, some frozen to death in almost 'natural' positions
– sitting around a non-existent fire, sleeping rolled up, or even
leaning on their guns. Odd shapes, unrecognisable under the snow. A
silence. Nothing moves. Into this comes PILS. He stands, lost. Slowly
he looks around. He spots something, and with a delicacy almost
unhuman, he moves toward it. Finally, he stands above a body. He
regards it. Time drifts. He takes a knife from his belt, and with
brutal speed begins to slice and hack at the dead body.*

PILS: Staring at me **staring** didn't expect that eh shit I'll
    wipe clean the smugness watch your face slid right off
    your head **fracture your nonchalance** look opening up
    a second mouth gaping red mouth red hell-hole still
    staring at me **staring at me** burst the sight burst it
    burst it

(*PILS stabs at the body's eye and pulls it from its socket. He regards it awhile. TORZHOK enters and regards PILS.*)

TORZHOK: I think, though I am no expert on these matters, that you will not find much of a fight with that particular gentleman. (*PILS turns to regard TORZHOK, still with the eye on the end of his knife.*) I could have passed on, certainly, yes, certainly you would never have noticed, being engrossed, yes, how quaint, 'engrossed', 'gross', yes, gross, with all its associations: repulsive, vulgar, rude, unacceptable, though could profit fit, I wonder, profit, maybe you are stealing from the unfortunate chap, which would make the act gross gross, if you see what I mean, repulsive profit, although a case could be made that all profit is gross, one way or another **I talk too much** yes, know it, too much, a symptom of nerves, perhaps, perhaps not, perhaps perhaps...why?

PILS: Found a frozen smile on the ground, tossed away, negligent, to lose a smile when they are in so short order...don't you think?

TORZHOK: I think, there is no manner of barbarity I cannot imagine, although some cultures, alien to us to be sure, although we must seem alien to them, thus, humans can be aliens, or indeed, we are all aliens to some extent, alienated from nature, to be sure, some would say our souls, yes, our souls are strange to us, stranger souls, yes indeed, although I don't think I have seen such a stranger soul than yours...

PILS: Does that always happen?

TORZHOK: What, precisely?

PILS: You start somewhere and go through the crazy forest to end up where you started from.

TORZHOK: Isn't that, in a manner of speaking, life, that is, we start as nothing return to nothing, the womb and tomb are both silent.

PILS: Are you saying my mother's cunt is a grave?

TORZHOK: Not quite, but of course the Elizabethans viewed intercourse as a small death, the ejection of sperm, naturally into the vagina, although strictly speaking, not necessarily the vagina, for, as I understand it, all forms of sex were practised, and performed, in those times, indeed all times, sex it seems is our one stable human trait, though not exclusively human, for as we know, animals, yes, and even plants, although obviously plants need help, bees and such like, and I have often wondered if bees actually know that they are helping a sex act, a multi-species orgy of kinds, and –

(*PILS hits TORZHOK, who collapses to the ground.*)

PILS: Had to do that – yes, had to – your speech – like a flood of poison gas – enveloped me – suffocated – like insidious death – slips in when you listen – only you don't listen anymore – just takes over – fucking hell, *I'm* doing it now!

TORZHOK: In such circumstances, this shouldn't matter, but I feel, strange, but yes, I feel as if I am going to cry, not through pain you understand, no, not that, but pride, hurt pride, amazing that something you can't touch can be hurt.

PILS: Who the fuck are you?

TORZHOK: Torzhok, poet, although I have yet to write anything, which technically doesn't make me a poet, although it is about feeling, poetry is feeling and I feel like a poet, which makes me a poet –

PILS: (*PILS hits TORZHOK again.*) Apologies – no, seriously – apologies – I don't – your words – I – **just have to hit you** –

TORZHOK: Are you a censor, or a critic, the same thing really, same result, the physical enactment of the censorship of art, of –

PILS: **I'm fucking warning you!**

TORZHOK: Quite.

PILS: Better! So, poet, eh? Must be a snob –

TORZHOK: Hardly –

PILS: No normal man would waste his time writing shitty poetry, I mean, come on! No, a snob…worth something I expect.

TORZHOK: If my father is to be believed, all poetry is
  worthless, especially love poetry, I see no reason for
  such a stance, although my father –
PILS: Love! Fuck me!
TORZHOK: Why not love?
PILS: Love is about slavish devotion, cherishing and
  adoring and years of service and protecting and culling
  your own soul for a smile and still being ignored
  trampled underfoot in the haste to taste some other and
  watching the destruction of the patter of my heart **just so
  that she can be hurt** –
TORZHOK: Don't understand, a woman, lust perhaps –
PILS: Like some whore yer wanna know 'bout them lust
  lust that's what they wish to fuck not me kept pure pure
  blood I'd never smelt their dripping dripping cunts and
  played their teases and games and legs and softness
  velvet veneer skin and glances and eyes **how they kill
  us with eyes** the things they say twisting in the brain
  and churning and freezing out logic and sense walked
  miles to avoid the spell of cunt and eyes and dizzy and
  rapid beat-beat-beat heart rhythm dislocated and love
  fuck love how it rasps under the skin slicing blue hate
  feet on broken glass oh the repellent attraction black lust
  white love all the same all the same I could have won
  her the stars but even that yes that baubles in mud never
  enough never ever enough I wanna slit their screaming
  souls open and make them kiss death **so much for cunt
  what the fuck do you know**
TORZHOK: Just…how unhappy you are…
PILS: (*PILS pulls out a pistol.*) Take this knife…and eat the
  fucking thing…
  (*PILS levels the gun at TORZHOK's head. Time.
  TORZHOK, wide-eyed with fear, closes his eyes and puts the
  eyeball into his mouth. He tries to chew, quickly, and tries to
  swallow but eventually vomits.*)
  See what love can do? That's a lesson, Mr Poet.

Scene Five

A huge artillery fight. NAPOLEON is bellowing out his song, and dancing a petit four. He comes across a WOUNDED MAN, who is attempting to crawl slowly across the stage. NAPOLEON observes him a while, still singing.

NAPOLEON: Farewell and adieu
to you fair Spanish ladies
Farewell and adieu to you ladies of Spain
For we received orders
for to sail back to Boston
And soon never more
will we see you again.
(A pause of contemplation.)
Bastard Spaniards!
(NAPOLEON grabs the WOUNDED MAN and hauls him up into a sitting position. NAPOLEON begins to recite a speech directly to the WOUNDED MAN.)
'Those men whom Nature had not hardened against all chances of fate and fortune seemed shaken; they lost their cheerfulness and good humour, and saw ahead of them nothing but disaster and catastrophe. Those on whom she had bestowed superior powers kept up their spirits and normal disposition, seeing in the various ordeals a challenge to win new glory.'
(He contemplates this awhile, then bursts out laughing. He drops the WOUNDED MAN who slumps to the floor. NAPOLEON weeps with laughter. NEY bursts in, stops shocked, and regards NAPOLEON. NAPOLEON sees NEY, and tries to stop laughing.)
I know...laughing amidst annihilation...hardly fitting... I know...hardly...at all... **God's bollocks, Ney, yer gotta laugh!**
(NAPOLEON laughs again.)

NEY: My Lord, the Russians approach...we must leave at once!

NAPOLEON: *(Indicates the WOUNDED MAN.)* This man...who is he? **Yer gotta laugh!**

NEY: My command of the rearguard has shrunk to five hundred men. The Russians snap at our heels. I fend them off during the day with a few rounds of artillery then a quick scamper to the next position. At night I find a hillock and set up my defences. They seem content to allow to do this. They seem content... **I do find their contentment a pisser!** Now a surprise attack. **Hardly fucking fair in the circumstances!**

(*NAPOLEON sighs. Loud gunfire.*)

NAPOLEON: Will you stay with me a while?

NEY: What? Can't you hear all this?

NAPOLEON: Just to talk –

NEY: **The guns, man**! Oh, Christ, you are not going to bang on about how lonely you are, are you? **Tired of the loneliness of genius!**

NAPOLEON: Not lonely – fucking bored!

(*Artillery shells land close by. NAPOLEON regards the WOUNDED MAN.*)

You don't like me, do you, Ney?

NEY: Well, I –

NAPOLEON: **Obvious as day!**

NEY: No... I don't...

NAPOLEON: Like most of them –

NEY: I don't think –

NAPOLEON: If the king came back they would flock to him! Mark that! You, like the rest, use me as a ladder to success.

NEY: We have to go –

NAPOLEON: Why do you fight for me, Ney?

NEY: What? I am a soldier, I fight where ordered.

NAPOLEON: And a good one, too. Ney, the world is full of starving dogs, each ripping and clawing their way to the top, only the way is brutal and savage – to reach the summit one must not think, just act, and act with barbarity, even then you wait for the slicing that will tear you apart. No rest, Ney, no rest, just barbarity.

NEY: Is that why we are here, in this God-forsaken place?

NAPOLEON: If not me, someone else.

NEY: And all the suffering?

(*NAPOLEON squats by the wounded man, who is still crawling across the stage. NAPOLEON produces a small knife.*)

NAPOLEON: Like snow, it drifts, and settles, and melts away.

(*NAPOLEON casually stabs the WOUNDED MAN in the leg. The WOUNDED MAN screams in pain and tries to crawl faster. NEY is both horrified and fascinated.*)

The atrocities committed in my name! History will not judge these men, it will judge me.

(*He stabs again.*)

The burden of mania!

(*NAPOLEON laughs. The WOUNDED MAN collapses, exhausted and dying. Gunfire all around.*)

They are saying my son has been taken to Austria. That Austria is barred to me. This hole...

NEY: (*Angry.*) **Power is the caprice of childishness** –

NAPOLEON: I have this hole...inside...filling with fear...and drip-drip it will fill and spill over the brim and drown me...fear...

NEY: We stumble in rout to rise and butcher Austrians –

NAPOLEON: (*Erupts in violence, stabbing the WOUNDED MAN again and again.*) I will exterminate the lice burn and burn and scythe this way and that and punish them stamp on them till the colours came out again and again I will remove their stain from the tortured earth I will chew holes in the fabric of their creation as if they had never existed **I will annihilate everything** –

NEY: Enough!

NAPOLEON: (*He weakens suddenly, all energy spent. The guns are silent temporarily.*) Tell me...tell me...

NEY: (*Confused and scared.*) What...tell you what?

NAPOLEON: Something...normal...

NEY: I...what?

NAPOLEON: Something simple...something that needs no explanation... **Now!**

NEY: (*Struggling.*) I... I...bird-song early with the pale flag of dawn rising and she's asleep and I sit watching her frozen with fear that she won't wake but my love stirs and butterflies dance around her lips and sighs and whispers and she opens her vast eyes and the meticulous chaotic perfection of her is awake and it is dawn and the slightest move shivers me and I long to brush away the tumbling playful lock of hair from her cheek but she turns the eternity of eyes upon me and I look away shamed to have been caught and her laughter is like a bell and it is dawn...

(*NAPOLEON moves to NEY and holds him. Silence. NAPOLEON shakes, but it is laughter. Great gusts of it explode from him. He moves away from NEY and falls to the ground in hysterics. He wipes tears from his eyes, and tries to speak to the stricken NEY through his laughter.*)

NAPOLEON: The bravest of the brave...the mightiest soldier in France... the warrior-prince...oh my...oh my... 'little butterflies'...what was it? Oh yes, 'her vast eyes'! (*More laughter.*) Oh Ney, you don't half cheer me up...**stuff your half-wit mumblings – away!**

(*NEY turns to leave, but NAPOLEON stops him, now in complete control.*)

Wait! Take the third Dragoons, they have no horse left, but good men – they'll help you with the Russians. And send my carriage. Go!

(*NEY exits stiff with anger and NAPOLEON returns to contemplating the WOUNDED MAN and the gunfire returns even closer.*)

Scene Six

A dressing station. Wounded men lie about everywhere. All are unattended, since the DOCTOR operates on OUDINOT. THE DEAD perform the Death Ritual, and take men who die into their ranks. They chant, whisper, and echo words from the play. TORZHOK is aware of them and is fascinated by their movements. OUDINOT is in great discomfit, and occasionally screams as the DOCTOR attempts to find the piece of shell lodged in OUDINOT's chest. OUDINOT labours to breath throughout, yet strangely, he is distant. ARNOUX and PILS stand, holding OUDINOT down. TORZHOK is trying talking to OUDINOT. Gunfire in the distance.

TORZHOK: History, Marshal Oudinot, lurches around us, no longer in control of any one man, or set of men, or indeed, of humanity, of course I exclude nature, although one could make a case that this winter dictates events now, but not consciously, it is absurd to think that some clouds actively seek to –

ARNOUX: Who is this fool?!

PILS: (*To the DOCTOR.*) For fuck sakes, get on with it!

DOCTOR: I can't find it! It's a mess in here! **Hold him straighter!**

OUDINOT: Her multi-coloured eyes – sun dazzling through snow-flakes –

TORZHOK: Put succinctly, were does the ordinary man fit in? What does he seek? Glory? If so, what kind? Medals? Fortune? What motivates him? His country? His Emperor? I don't understand why they are here. (*TORZHOK notices THE DEAD.*) Have you not seen this –

OUDINOT: **Agh!** To hold you – to be wrapped in your colours –

PILS: Sorry, my lord, but this **deluge of words** –

TORZHOK: And I understand conscription, but even so, they fight ferociously –

DOCTOR: What the hell is this? (*The DOCTOR produces a bone.*)

PILS: Shouldn't you know that?

DOCTOR: Before this war, I used to attend to ladies, mostly of the lower part, if you know what I mean.

PILS: Cunt-Doctor – that's all we need!

OUDINOT: (*In great pain.*) Come to me again with smiles and fragility – such glances –

TORZHOK: I have seen incredible things – barbarism, courage, anger, selflessness – but it isn't glory they are fighting for. No indeed. (*Again he notices THE DEAD.*) What is this –

PILS: Then you know nothing about the average Frenchman.

TORZHOK: That could be true, but I would suggest that it is what I have seen that makes me convinced, although I will admit that I may have missed certain sights, possibly no one could actually see everything, unless of course they were in a balloon, now that is interesting – (*PILS, unable to take any more of TORZHOK's talk, leaps at him and punches him to the ground.*)

PILS: I know – I know what you're gonna say – but – fuck me – he drives you mad!

OUDINOT: (*Half delirious with pain.*) And my heart...your rainbow smiles...with eyes of colours...sing to me again...
(*PILS returns to OUDINOT and holds him down. TORZHOK gets up rubbing his jaw, and resumes.*)

TORZHOK: I have seen real glory in the simplest of things. A man calming a young boy down after an attack; another man sharing his food with an injured comrade; soldiers sparing their enemies, the list is endless – but a duty that is neither noticed nor necessary. I say! Look!
(*THE DEAD begin to gather around OUDINOT. TORZHOK is nervous.*)

OUDINOT: (*Gasping.*) Forgiveness – quest of the tainted – stained –

TORZHOK: (*Pointing at THE DEAD.*) Humanity shining in the mire – **who are these men and why** –
(*ARNOUX steps across to TORZHOK and grabs him.*)

ARNOUX: Leave them – no concern to you – the balance tilts this way and that – men – just men – leave them
(*ARNOUX watches TORZHOK carefully and then returns to OUDINOT.*)

TORZHOK: (*Wary, but still watching THE DEAD.*) Poetry's duty is to capture the beauty of the soul – all around me, I do not see the glory of history, nor the savagery, but rather the glory of humanity. That is what I wish to capture in words, for without written words, that glory is lost in the moment.

DOCTOR: I had thought poetry was the recounting of glorious deeds and the tales of heroes. What you suggest is the ordinary, the mundane, the banal.

(*THE DEAD appear to be taking OUDINOT. TORZHOK points, trying to warn the group.*)

TORZHOK: Eh .. Look here, they…eh…

ARNOUX: **The balance** – be quiet –

TORZHOK: Oh…

DOCTOR: Well? What about banality then?

TORZHOK: That – that is the glory I seek for.

PILS: Only a bleeding Russian could come up with such balls.

DOCTOR: Got the fucker!

(*THE DEAD drift away.*)

Not all of it, but the biggest piece! What about that, Marshal?

(*The DOCTOR shows OUDINOT the fragment of shell. OUDINOT groans. TORZHOK watches THE DEAD go, fascinated.*)

Excellent, excellent! A drink first, then cover him up, Arnoux. We won't sew up the hole till later – more stuff in there. I will look in again tomorrow. Pils, help me with my instruments.

(*The DOCTOR and PILS gather up the medical instruments, and the DOCTOR exits. ARNOUX, after giving OUDINOT a drink, bandages him. OUDINOT recovers somewhat.*)

TORZHOK: (*Watching the last of THE DEAD exit.*) If only I had my notebook –

OUDINOT: (*Wane and pale, struggling with his words.*) I heard words…poetry…screaming… Pils, feed the man.

PILS: (*To OUDINOT.*) He is mine, remember? My, and my sister's pay off – remember?

OUDINOT: Naturally.

(*PILS and TORZHOK exit. A silence whereupon ARNOUX continues to tend to OUDINOT.*)

ARNOUX: That skunk, Pils, steals from you –

OUDINOT: Know it –

ARNOUX: Uses your name for advancement –

OUDINOT: Know it –

ARNOUX: Spreads the worst tales about you –

OUDINOT: **Know it!**

ARNOUX: Let me bleed him –

OUDINOT: He...brother-in-law –

ARNOUX: Thousands die every die, what is one more pig?

OUDINOT: Look after the Russian...bring him to Paris...
I, personally...will reward you.

ARNOUX: You will live, I take it?

OUDINOT: Unfortunately –

ARNOUX: **Stuff the romantic self-pity!** Christ, myth-
building in this carnage – nothing changes – **shame on
you!**

OUDINOT: It's just...when I get back... The Emperor may
have lost an empire, but... I much more...she will be
gone.

ARNOUX: At Neckerau, surrounded by screaming
Austrians, you cut five times, I had to pound you into
surrender – the brave death was it? **Enshrined in
immortality!** Prick!

OUDINOT: Why do you...hate me?

ARNOUX: Nineteen years of service together.

OUDINOT: We've...come a long way –

ARNOUX: Yes, you to Marshal, me to Sergeant – bitter?
Me? I took the bridge at Morlautend not you! I should
have been promoted, not you!

OUDINOT: Took it together –

ARNOUX: I was first –

OUDINOT: Still this hatred –

ARNOUX: I remained Sergeant, not you!

OUDINOT: Nineteen years –

ARNOUX: I still live in the moment! No escape! Twisting
as daggers in the skin! Even in dreams! **Not you!**
(*ARNOUX punches OUDINOT's wound, and OUDINOT
squeals like a pig. ARNOUX is instantly ashamed.*)
You make me do horrid things...all the time, horrid
things...shame on you...
(*Silence awkwardly descends.*)

171

She told me…you and her…as I lay in the next room…injured from the bridge at Morlautend…she told me…everything…

OUDINOT: (*Struggling.*) Arnoux…no excuses…not even sorry…but time bleaches so many things…**nineteen years** –

ARNOUX: I will bring your Russian home safely – then we talk.

OUDINOT: Of what?

ARNOUX: I want my life back.

(*ARNOUX exits. OUDINOT stares after him.*)

Scene Seven

A frozen road somewhere. EUGENIE enters followed closely by an OFFICER. The OFFICER is clearly pestering EUGENIE, and as she talks to him she looks around, as if for help.

OFFICER: Madame, I have no idea what you think my intentions are, but let me assure you that I am an officer of the Third Chasseurs de Garde. This is no place for a lady of your obvious breeding, and thus, I am duty bound to offer you assistance whether you accept it or no. Please, let me lead you to the main road, and thus, to safety.

EUGENIE: Whilst I appreciate your kind offer, once again I must state that I wait for my husband and his entourage. I am not lost, nor indeed needing of help, so thank you kindly, but please, do not let me hold up your journey any longer.

OFFICER: Then, my dear Madame, I shall wait with you until your husband arrives – it is the least I could do.

EUGENIE: I know this sounds slightly ludicrous, but my husband is of the jealous type, and I do not think he would take it too kindly if he arrived and found you here.

OFFICER: But, Madame, I am an officer of the Garde, how could you husband place the slightest suspicion on me?

(*EUGENIE attempts to turn away, but slips on the snow. The OFFICER immediately rushes to her help, and catches her by the hand. EUGENIE reacts furiously and slaps the OFFICER.*)

EUGENIE: For God sake's, why don't you just go!

(*A moment's awkward silence. The OFFICER stares at EUGENIE.*)

I cannot apologise enough, my dear sir; I am so worried about my husband that –

(*The OFFICER punches EUGENIE in the face, and she falls both stunned and badly hurt. The OFFICER advances upon her.*)

OFFICER: Now tell me how sorry you are, you stupid fucking bitch. Christ, you're just the same as any other whore. Think that dirty rancid hole of yours makes me go weak at the knees? Stupid bitch.

(*The OFFICER now stands over EUGENIE. She is dazed, but tries to crawl away. The OFFICER catches her and tries to lift her up.*)

Come on, bitch, let's dance – .

(*EUGENIE hits the OFFICER again and again, but the blows are weak. The OFFICER hits her again, hard on the face. EUGENIE falls, now unconscious.*)

Stupid girl. Now, let's see what you have, my pretty one.

(*The OFFICER searches EUGENIE's clothes and finds a purse. He tries to take off her wedding ring, but fails swearing. Angered, he sits back at looks at EUGENIE. Slowly, he glides his hand up EUGENIE's leg, beyond the hem of her dress and towards her inside thigh.*)

Well, here's a nice warm place. All that electric fur, purring away like a sleeping cat. I bet you even splash cologne on that. Shall we find out?

(*The OFFICER moves between EUGENIE's legs and begins to lift her dress up. Before the OFFICER can move, GABRIELLE rushes on and hits the OFFICER on the head with a thick tree trunk. The OFFICER falls over EUGENIE in a heap. He tries to get up, but GABRIELLE attacks him. They tussle, but again GABRIELLE hits him with the tree*) *trunk. Finally, unable to regain the initiative, the OFFICER turns and flees, pursued by GABRIELLE. Silence passes overhead. GABRIELLE returns, minus the tree trunk, although now covered in blood. She shouts back at the OFFICER.*)

GABRIELLE: Pig-fuck – all the same – **think that's a weapon?** Now you suck my weapon to hell and back! Pig-fuck…

(*GABRIELLE turns her attention to EUGENIE, who still lies unconscious. Gently rubbing snow onto EUGENIE's head, GABRIELLE manages to wake EUGENIE up.*)

There we go, me old girl, back to the living – although who the fuck would want to come back here and live, eh?

EUGENIE: What… I…what…**get off me at once!**

(*EUGENIE sits up and pushes GABRIELLE off her. GABRIELLE ends up covered in snow.*)

Get off me! Who are you? Where is that horrid man? Go away! Go away I said! Go away or I'll…

GABRIELLE: Ah! At last – reason returns – knew it would – nice to see you Mr Reason – it's been a long time.

(*GABRIELLE gets up and bows, then falls back down laughing.*)

EUGENIE: Who…just who are you?

GABRIELLE: Gabrielle Arnoux, my lady. Mother of eight – although six are dead – seamstress – although unemployed – fabulous drinker of brandy – although sober now – and ex-whore – although sadly the possessor of a sown up cunt. And you?

EUGENIE: That is none of your business! My, what…just go away! I am leaving – do not follow me, you…you…

GABRIELLE: Yes, spoilt for insults to throw at me – don't worry – most are – old hag – drunkard – whore – take your pick –

EUGENIE: (*Getting up.*) I won't lower myself. Now, if you'll excuse me, I am going!

GABRIELLE: No you're not!

EUGENIE: Now look here –

GABRIELLE: On that road, over there, the French army is in bleeding, chaotic retreat – and on that road over there, the Russkis are fucking anything French – in more ways than one – you're going nowhere – unless you want some more fisticuffs with a sex-starved pig-fuck. Well?

EUGENIE: (*Hesitating.*) I... I... I shall stay here...but you must move away.

GABRIELLE: And why on earth would I want to do that?

EUGENIE: Look, I don't want to cause trouble, but I...

(*EUGENIE sways and has to sit.*)

GABRIELLE: That'll be the bash on the head – or maybes you're starving – you look like a bundle of bones.

EUGENIE: Just tired, thank you.

GABRIELLE: I've got food in this bag and a tree trunk we could burn for heat over there – bloody, yes, but it'll do. We're both too tired to go anywhere so fuck it all: let's be friends!

EUGENIE: I...yes...why not? You could have hurt me by now if you had wanted to...and that...man, stole my purse ... I have nothing now.

GABRIELLE: Look, darling, we're not in a melodramatic Italian novel now, you know! You're still alive, got some food, heat, and a new friend! Fuck me, what more could anyone want?

(*EUGENIE laughs.*)

EUGENIE: You're right, I apologise. May I introduce myself: I am Eugenie Oudinot, the Duchesse de Reggio.

(*GABRIELLE's face blanches.*)

Are you all right? You look pale!

GABRIELLE: Fine – fine... I thought I heard a ghost form the past – but ghosts – pah – November mist – they soon melt away.

EUGENIE: I suspect you want to know why I am out here?

GABRIELLE: You're a woman – you must be running away from something – God – I hope that wasn't your boyfriend over there – let us just say: he won't yodel again.

EUGENIE: Not running from, but to my husband. He has been hurt and I have come here to find him, and take him home.

GABRIELLE: My! Iron behind the lace! Good for you, girl. Why, we have something in common! I too seek my husband!

EUGENIE: Has he been hurt?

GABRIELLE: Yes, my lady; in the heart…in the heart – trying to make good again – always trying to make good lately – it's like tearing a brick in half…

EUGENIE: I'm sorry…

GABRIELLE: Don't be – tonight we talk – tomorrow – sisters in arms – we set forth to find our husbands – oh, before I forget – here this is yours.

(*GARIELLE throws EUGENIE's purse to EUGENIE. GABRIELLE begins to sing as she brings out some food from her bag. EUGENIE smiles at her.*)

Scene Eight

Another part of the road. Carnage. Clearly a battle has taken place here. Dead bodies abound. Shuffling into this morass comes a soldier, the FATHER, and his daughter, BERNADETTE. They stop to take in the horror. The FATHER slumps down, staring out into the desolation around them. BERNADETTE systematically searches the dead for food, money, wood, weapons, etc. The wind howls.

FATHER: Wonder wha' 'appened to the lads? Can't be all dead.

BERNADETTE: Why not? Everyone else is.

FATHER: Trained wes were. Bloody good men. Can't all be dead.

BERNADETTE: (*Finding a small pistol.*) Would this be any good?

FATHER: Fancy bein' caught in the open by cavalry. Basic mistake. 'acked to bleedin' pieces we was. **Feel ashamed I ran!**

BERNADETTE: You're alive, that's all that matters –

FATHER: Wha' good is tha' to anyone?

BERNADETTE: Listen, I lost a mother and I ain't gonna lose a father. Now come over here and help me. It'll be dark soon.

FATHER: If yer mum could see us now – scavengers. Crow-blacks, tha's what we call 'em: crow-blacks.

BERNADETTE: (*Looking through her spoils.*) No food, but a few coins. Just gotta find a place to spend 'em now.

FATHER: I ain't done a good job in lookin' after yer, 'ave I? Mum would be furious.

BERNADETTE: You're a soldier, you go places, I follow; it's no one's fault. It'd be the same with mother.

FATHER: She'd find sum food –

BERNADETTE: I'm doing the best I can!

FATHER: I didn't mean – it's my fault – tha's wha' I'm tryin' to say…

BERNADETTE: (*Alert.*) Soldiers are coming – quick!
(*The FATHER grabs his gun and cocks it. BERNADETTE stands behind him. Two French SOLDIERS bundle onstage, both looking like dishevelled tramps. Both groups look at each other for a while. Finally.*)

SOLDIER 1: French uniform – yer gotta be one of us.

FATHER: Fifteenth Light Infantry – yer?

SOLDIER 2: Second Dragoons…lost our 'orses.

FATHER: We's got nuthin'.

SOLDIER 1: Nor's we.

FATHER: Tha's fine, then.

SOLDIER 2: It's fine.

SOLDIER 1: Yer gonna put tha' gun down?

SOLDIER 2: It's fine, like yer said.

FATHER: It's fine?

SOLDIER 2: It's fine.

FATHER: Fine then.
(*The FATHER lowers his gun.*)

BERNADETTE: Father!

FATHER: It's fine, like theys said.
(*A moment of indecision wafts around.*)

SOLDIER 1: Can't stand all day…ain't on guard duty now.
(*SOLDIER 1 and 2 sit.*)

SOLDIER 2: Silly all this – look at us – friends yet…well, look at us!

FATHER: Aye, silly.

(*The FATHER sits down next to the SOLDIERS. BERNADETTE keeps her distance.*)

Fought at Austerlitz – no troubles then.

SOLDIER 1: Good days then…good days.

SOLDIER 2: Caught meself a general – got promoted to sergeant –

SOLDIER 1: Lost the rank for bein' drunk on duty, though.

SOLDIER 2: That's war – up 'n' down –

(*SOLDIER 1 hits the FATHER in the head with his rifle butt. The FATHER tumbles over, dazed. SOLDIER 2 leaps up and grabs the FATHER, pulling him up. SOLDIER 1 goes to butt the FATHER again, when BERNADETTE produces a pistol and levels it at the SOLDIERS.*)

BERNADETTE: Put 'im down! Now!

SOLDIER 1: She wouldn' –

SOLDIER 2: It ain't loaded –

BERNADETTE: Who wants to find out for sure?

(*The SOLDIERS think about this, but then look at each other. With an unspoken agreement, they both advance upon BERNADETTE.*)

BERNADETTE: I'm warning you! I'll fucking do one of you!

(*Just as the SOLDIERS get close enough to jump at BERNADETTE, voices are heard off-stage: Russian voices. The SOLDIERS freeze.*)

SOLDIER 1: Shit! Russkis!

SOLDEIR 2: Look! A whole group of them!

SOLDIER 1: Fuck it! I'm outta 'ere!

(*The SOLDIERS exit quickly, ignoring BERNADETTE. BERNADETTE's front crumbles, and she begins to pant through fear. Her FATHER moans.*)

BERNADETTE: Quickly, father! The Russians!

FATHER: Can't bleedin' think straight – gone all dizzy, like.

(*BERNADETTE tries to lift her FATHER, but can't. She thinks desperately.*)

BERNADETTE: Father – we'll have to pretend to be dead. Can you do that? Father?

FATHER: Wha'? Dead! Wha' if we –

BERNADETTE: There's no time! Can you do that?

FATHER: Aye – come on then! Put yer 'ead under me coat.

(*BERNADETTE and the FATHER arrange themselves on the ground. A moment or two. Very slowly, three RUSSIAN SOLDIERS enter. They are very cautious, and begin to check the dead bodies around them. They search some, and one RUSSIAN SOLDIER begins to search BERNADETTE and her FATHER. Just as the RUSSIAN SOLDIER begins his search of the couple, another RUSSIAN SOLDIER shouts – he has found a FRENCH SOLDIER alive. All three RUSSIAN SOLDIERS converge upon the FRENCH SOLDIER, and during the ensuing search, argument, and anger, the three RUSSIAN SOLDIERS club the FRENCH SOLDIER to death. A silence. They search the dead body, and find a purse. Happy with themselves, they exit. Moments pass. The FATHER tentatively stirs, then gets up. BERNADETTE follows.*)

FATHER: Fuckin' close, tha' was!

(*BERNADETTE starts to cry. Her FATHER cuddles her.*)
It's all right, lass. All right now. They's gone 'n' we're together. It's all right now. All right.

Scene Nine

Another part of the frozen road. ARNOUX and TORZHOK stagger on-stage. Both men are exhausted and somehow have acquired many layers of clothes. ARNOUX appears grim-faced, head bent against the wind. TORZHOK, although slow, talks with an air of nonchalance.

TORZHOK: One cannot deny it; one more step is one less step; simple logic really; and the beauty of that logic is that it doesn't matter how big or indeed, small the step is; it is still one step less; unless, of course, you step side-wards, or indeed, backwards; however, if that were the case, then I would suggest it wasn't a step; no, for, implicitly of course, a step suggests forward momentum; thus, we walk the line to paradise – how strange! Did I really say 'paradise'? Of course, I meant Paris; or did I?

(*ARNOUX signals for them to halt. ARNOUX takes a water bottle out from under his coat, opens it, and tries to drink; the water is frozen. TORZHOK watches him closely.*)
I hope you don't mind me saying this, but I did warn you that the water would still be frozen; putting amongst your clothes would do no good; no, indeed, no good; your body temperature itself has lowered; the skin, despite the multiple layers of clothes, is cold; the blood contracts the veins so it won't have to flow near the skin; it is basic physics that as the blood flows near the skin, it loses heat; thus, in times such as this, the veins constrict and the blood flows nearer the bone; keeping our internal temperature up, but out outer temperature, cold; in a way, we are like a pavlova – no, actually, the opposite to one, for, as you know –
(*Two FRENCH SOLDIERS enter. They spot ARNOUX and TORZHOK and rise their guns.*)
SOLDIER 1: Stop right there!
SOLDIER 2: Well, well. Looks like we got ourselves a couple of Russkis! Hands up, then!
(*TORZHOK puts his hands up, but ARNOUX does not. The two FRENCH SOLDIERS become uncertain.*)
SOLDIER 1: You heard the man!
SOLDIER 2: Funny fuck, ain't he?
(*Slowly, ARNOUX pulls two pistols out from his clothing, and amid the panic and shouts of the two FRENCH SOLDIERS, ARNOUX shoots them both deliberately. TORZHOK, is horrified and scared witless.*)
TORZHOK: What in... I mean...how could...do you realise they were French?
(*ARNOUX makes no reply, but instead begins to search the two dead FRENCH SOLDIERS.*)
They didn't fire...proof, if any be needed, that they weren't your enemy ... How could you do that? Shoot them in cold blood?
ARNOUX: They would have killed us, given the chance.
TORZHOK: But why didn't they... I mean...you weren't exactly slow about producing those things.

ARNOUX: Look at their muskets. To save the firing mechanism from freezing, they have covered them with grease and wadding – they can't fire. You would need to take all this crap off first. Stupid fucks!

TORZHOK: But why did you kill them? You could have just simply – let them go.

ARNOUX: If I hadn't killed them, I wouldn't have found this – (*ARNOUX holds up a flask of wine.*) or this. (*He holds up some meat wrapped in cloth.*) Now we can eat and drink tonight without wasting our own supplies.

TORZHOK: Has it come to this?

ARNOUX: Listen, you want to live, I want to live, this is how it's done! Got that! Nothing is going to get in the way of me getting you back to Paris! Nothing! Even your prattling won't, and by God, how I want to do you harm. But I won't, I'll get you back instead and no amount of this filth will stand in my way. Got that?

TORZHOK: But think of the thousands of men who have died in this war – these two killings are senseless in that context –

ARNOUX: We walk alone – that's all.

TORZHOK: Once it breaks down, it'll never mend again.

ARNOUX: Preach your wisdom to the crows. I stand between life and death for you – be grateful.

TORZHOK: Arnoux, listen to me. You are a decent man, do not lose that decency –

ARNOUX: I have been fighting for twenty years! Twenty years! What's this word 'decency'? Don't know it. All I know is war. **War is holy!** Ripping someone's throat out is more satisfying than sex. You ought to feel it, just once. Then you'll know life! You'll feel the difference between life and death, and then know what all this is about. Your poetry? Fuck it! It means nothing! It saves nothing! It changes nothing! War does! War is life! **War is holy!**

TORZHOK: All I see is loneliness in your eyes...and fear.

ARNOUX: (*Angry.*) Fear! **Fear!** Does this look like fear? (*ARNOUX hits TORZHOK, who crumples to the floor.*)

Or this?
(*ARNOUX kicks TORZHOK brutally.*)
Or this?
(*Again.*)
This?
(*ARNOUX loses control and repeatedly kicks TORZHOK until he is exhausted. Finally ARNOUX stops, panting and shaking with anger. He spits on TORZHOK and goes over to the wine flask and takes a long drink from it. He eyes TORZHOK who has not moved since the beating. Reluctantly, ARNOUX goes over to TORZHOK and checks on his condition.*)
Fuck!
(*ARNOUX packs away his gear and goes over to TORZHOK and picks him up like a child.*)
That's it, my poet, you rest. I'll do the donkey work. That's how it is, art riding on the back of reality. Enjoy the rest while you can, Mr Poet.
(*ARNOUX carries TORZHOK off.*)

Scene Ten

A cabin. OUDINOT and PILS wait.

OUDINOT: There had been a time when... I don't mean that...no...soldiers follow the call...yes... I have travelled so many places...so far...yet each step away is another step back...home...a place of solace...what I wanted...no...not that either... I loved her, Pils –
(*PILS is silent.*)
I loved her –

PILS: **Heard It!** Yet, begging me pardon, your arse-holiness, but you have just the past tense: 'loved', and you still killed my nephew. Forgive if I want to stamp your lying body and crush you to red mush.

OUDINOT: I listened to others...lies and half-truths...her only nineteen...and me forty-four...who could blame her...position...money...glamour...she fell in love with that...not me –

PILS: If you believe that then – why are you such a cunt?
    She dies for you every moment you are absent, and you
    have been so very absent – have seen her hurt – her pain
    – horror beneath her eyes – those eyes you abused –
    destroyer of beauty –
OUDINOT: They said she –
PILS: 'They?' 'They?' Fuck 'they'. You have defiled
    innocence and destroyed love – you will burn – here, on
    this earth, and in eternity – I am the annihilator – I will
    scythe you – hack at you – cut you down like a disease –
    inflict...such things –
OUDINOT: You are right...time renounces mercy...so be
    it... I sought death in battle...no more...you are right...
    when the time comes...devour me with your hatred...and
    love – none of it – I am barren now...
    (*NAPOLEON, NEY, and the FATHER enter. NAPOLEON
    nods to OUDINOT. NEY keeps a watch on the FATHER.
    The FATHER stands before them. Around them rise THE
    DEAD. As the FATHER's story continues, THE DEAD begin
    to act it out in a ritualistic way, to the point, that as the
    FATHER goes on, THE DEAD become integrated with his
    story.*)
FATHER: The river Berezina is more than half frozen and
    below the sparkling ice the blue-cold water lethargically
    meanders and the weight of grey-mournful clouds
    resonates as snow sings silently and two bridges slice
    through the steel-cold skating heavy and colour drains
    white-white and dazzling precise death waits and all day
    as clocks tick-tock relentlessly streamed the French army
    organised flight forming-streaming-reforming forming-
    streaming-reforming forming-streaming-reforming on-
    and-on-and-on still they came tattered skeletons
    whispering ancient tales of glory amidst the carnage and
    the bustle in their eyes and lateness in their limbs and
    jagged breaths and discordant beat-beating of hearts and
    still they came forming-streaming-reforming forming-
    streaming-reforming and night like a hunter comes and
    the stars stare down like distant malevolent eyes and in

the stone-quiet they shuffle the thousand unalive relics
with starving desires and crippling purpose bundles of
decaying flesh rotting with every half-step and eyes as
nails and floatingly their souls this way and that tumble
and slide and down they crumble and drifting it comes
shaking biting inertia for the two spanning gates to
freedom are hushed now and only white flakes of
eternity aimlessly wander this way and that over the
unmoving dead wood yet no one stirs as if the merest
sight of escape is enough and long deep night indolently
passes by and with the pale flag dawn comes the
forming-streaming-reforming forming-streaming-
reforming and with hurry unforeseen they are over and
the last form to leave yet still the thousand bundles rest
sunning themselves white **and still they will not move**
and pleading and beating and begging remain ignored
and they stare through ice-eyes at nothing and haste is a
commodity long sold out when out of the white sounds
they come dark lizard-quick monsters and howling and
blood-needful with immediate lusts and splintered logic
and now the thousand-thousand bundles swirl and black-
dread seeps as tears and battle do they for the twin arcs
of solace an enormous pile of humanity laying siege to
the slender gateways of the bridges begun it did as those
in front pressed from those behind squeezed into the
efficiency of the span flake-by-flake tumbled and as the
press pressed tumble and fall and tramp-tramp and
trampled and stamped and others thrown into freezing
death and splish-splash-splosh the river feasted and the
throng initiated a dirge and wail and ghastly laments
now a low humming now mangled terrifying curses and
moans and screeches and bellows and some hacking their
forward with despair shoving hopelessness pushing rank
fear and splish-splash-splosh the river feasted women
among the floes holding cobalt-iced babes in their
drowning arms and then the first arc collapses leisurely
nauseatingly unhurried toying with catastrophe those on
it try to rout over those behind but those behind assail

forward and squeeze-squeeze-squeeze the fractured air out and splish-splash-splosh the river feasted and twice the honeyed swarm on the remaining arc of solace but bang-clatter-thud a horse dragged down and plunge the bundles and terror-shrieks resound and grunting driving passion for solace hollers in their ears and heaving bursting wood splinters and cracks and splish-splash-splosh the river feasted drowning and freezing and the magnanimous French Army with pride glowing from its eyes set fire to the last arc and the fragile thread of life explodes in horror and annihilation and death and swooping and darting comes the horseman descending and crushing shattering and dissolve before us the thousand-thousand bundles melting into white and fading colours and white-white as if they had never been and silence is the most powerful sound I have ever heard (*NAPOLEON, after an eon, walks to the FATHER and hits him.*)

NAPOLEON: I leave tonight...there is nothing here...nothing at all...
(*NAPOLEON exits.*)

End of Act One

ACT TWO

Scene One

Only a centre spot. THE DEAD are seen moving on the periphery of it. They intone THE SECOND PROLOGUE OF THE DEAD.

THE DEAD: Driftingly float they
    Whirling blown shrieks
    Driving this way and that
    White silence biting
    Now too stripped layers
    This moral that ethic
    And being worse for wear
    Moderation drip-drip wash away
    Irresistible morass
    Things come apart
    The blank moments
    Cracked and dissolving
    Aim skewered
    Hope bent out of shape
    And time tramp-tramp-tramps
    Precise howling fear
    Stalking colours
    We walk alone we walk alone
    One world outside
    A million within
    Bellowing life-greed
    And black-black sun
    The world frowning
    And insect crawl-crawl
    We walk alone we walk alone
    (THE DEAD finally come to a halt and become SOLDIERS heating themselves around an imaginary fire, in the spot. The wind howls. PILS bursts into the circle, a blur of movement and physical violence.)
PILS: Marshal outside – get out – get out – move
    yourselves – you – move –

(*PILS physical picks up men and hurls them out of the cabin.
He produces a pistol and threatens the men with it. He beats,
kicks, and abuses the SOLDIERS, who, too exhausted, do not
fight back, but rather, one by one, disappear from the spot.*)
Fucking get up – piss off, you – up – up – come on –
fuck off – **Marshal outside** –
(*Eventually PILS manages to clear the room. He exits and
swiftly returns with OUDINOT.*)

OUDINOT: Empty cabin...with a fire...how, Pils?

PILS: Don't ask...sit – Christ! The fire!
(*PILS rushes over to the fire and tries to keep it going.
OUDINOT, with considerable pain, sits.*)

OUDINOT: Even though...it will soon be morning... I
appreciate this gesture –

PILS: Don't fool yourself – you stay alive – I get my
money – then I take my sister away from you – don't
fool yourself.

OUDINOT: Still...perhaps I should sign something...in
case I die...you know, giving everything to you –

PILS: Won't have it! Bluff within bluff – **the treachery of
good intentions!** My sister loves you, fool that she is –
without a body, she will pine – mope around – **cunt
martyr!** No! You stay alive – face to face into her eyes:
you tell her.

OUDINOT: And so...stain innocence...so be it...

PILS: Fuck this fire! It's out – no more warmth here – we
wait till sunrise.

OUDINOT: I dreamed earlier...all the men I had
known...good men... I can still see them now...each and
every one... I sent them to their deaths...**death-bringer!**

PILS: You pig-fuck! You sit and wallow in your own
sentimental filth – dragging up the souls of giants to ease
your guilt – **is no sacrilege enough?**

OUDINOT: You allow me nothing –

PILS: Nothing!

OUDINOT: Then you will give me what I
seek...absolution.

IAIN LANDLES

PILS: I give you coals in the skin – pins in the eyes – I give you screaming eternal hate!

OUDINOT: Will you kill me…after…

PILS: Dead already – zombie.

OUDINOT: It's just…just that… I have a daughter…that's all…

PILS: Another pig-fuck…don't want to hear more guilt-stories –

OUDINOT: Not like that…just…**if it's going to be done, do it all!**

PILS: Have you fucked everyone? Is that it? Immortality through spunk?

OUDINOT: The young exist to make mistakes…remember what I came from –

PILS: I can still smell it –

OUDINOT: Things easier then … politics…none of it…**we knew the enemy**…seems as if even mirrors lie… I can't remember her face…only her smell…

PILS: Easy to recall shit –

OUDINOT: A room…a tavern somewhere – Roux's, behind the Bastille! Yes, Roux's…she served there…a young officer…in love with life and glory…oh, yes… I called her the 'broken one'…she had a club foot, but…can't remember her face…

PILS: Always the same! The aristos fucking the peasants – **no game, you know!**

OUDINOT: Smell her now…acrid, probing smell…she told me of the child when I came back… Italy, '92…she'd married…Light Infantry man…never saw the girl up close…watched her grow…from afar…from afar…

PILS: I smell the sun – up!

OUDINOT: Could you take a message –

PILS: Nothing! Understand! Nothing!

OUDINOT: I just thought…not her fault…would be nice…that's all…

(*PILS helps OUDINOT to get up. The lights slowly rise. Around the pair, the SOLDIERS sit dead – frozen. OUDINOT stares at them.*)

Are these...did we... I mean...is this...

PILS: Yes – your two minutes of warmth – the price,
Oudinot – the price!
(*The men slowly exit.*)

Scene Two

Twilight. THE DEAD hum a lament that echoes around the theatre.
They continue this throughout the scene. BERNADETTE sits by a
dead soldier. She is slowly skinning the man, peeling long strips of
his flesh off of his back. She, too, hums, concentrating on her job. She
places the strips into a small wooden bowl. She finishes as her
FATHER enters.

FATHER: No wood anywhere. Them trees is frozen, which
means I can' break the branches off – nah, no wood
anywhere.

BERNADETTE: We shall have to drink snow again, then.
Come, sit and eat.
(*The FATHER sits and BERNADETTE gives him a piece of*
flesh. He gnaws hungrily at it.)

FATHER: Good stuff this! 'ow do you find this?

BERNADETTE: It's getting old – salted meat, you know.

FATHER: But it tastes so fresh!

BERNADETTE: Don't talk now, just eat.

FATHER: Ain't you 'aving some?

BERNADETTE: I had mine earlier –

FATHER: Look, me darling, we 'ave to eat, you
understand?

BERNADETTE: I ate earlier, I just told you, didn't I?

FATHER: I checked over tha' 'ill – the road becomes
bigger – joins another road – lots of soldiers –

BERNADETTE: We should avoid them and keep going
through these fields.

FATHER: You think so?

BERNADETTE: Also, we should walk for three hours, then
an hour's rest, then walk for three hours.

FATHER: Three 'ours! A long time in this here snow 'n'
ice –
BERNADETTE: And it's a long way to France – you expect
us to fly there?
(*An awkward moment.*)
I'm sorry –
FATHER: Nah! It's my fault. If I was more of a man –
BERNADETTE: Not this again!
FATHER: But it's true –
BERNADETTE: Just be quiet and eat –
FATHER: You see?
(*They smile at one another. Silence.*)
You get tha' strength from your mother – she was a
strong lady – used to cuff 'er customers if they touched
her arse – (*He laughs.*) why, she once laid out a Dragoon
for groping 'er as she bent over the table – 'one up for
the light infantry', we shouted – such times.
BERNADETTE: Why did she stop working to follow you?
FATHER: I don't rightly know – in fact, I don't know why
she married me – 'ad 'er pick of any of the men – they
said she picked me only because she won a fortune on
the sweep-stake – I was twenty-five to one – an outsider!
It sounds 'bout right –
BERNADETTE: Maybe she picked you because you are
kind and gentle, and not horrid like the others.
FATHER: You shouldn't be so 'ard on the lads – war
changes things – those who were once decent men –
well, they change – 'n' when the wars finish – they
change back –
BERNADETTE: Do you really believe that?
FATHER: Gotta believe in something.
BERNADETTE: You could still paint, you know.
FATHER: Art shouldn't be sullied by all this – painting
plates – tha's what I love – an irrelevant detail – 'unting
scenes on a plate – but I like to believe theys add to the
enjoyment of the food – not important – no – not in
themselves – but all together – they mean something,
otherwise, why would we do it?

(*An exhausted SOLDIER enters, staggering. He half-collapses, half-sits. He looks up at BERNADETTE and her FATHER. The SOLDIER smiles. He lowers his head to his breast, and dies. Silence. THE DEAD lament.*)
Should we go...perhaps?

BERNADETTE: I do not think it is necessary to go.

FATHER: We'd better watch 'im –

BERNADETTE: (*Getting up and going over to the SOLDIER.*) Father, this man is dead.

FATHER: But – like tha' – 'e dies like tha'?

BERNADETTE: And all around us.

FATHER: Just to sit 'n' die – 'n' no one stirred 'n' nothing moved – just sat 'n' died.

BERNADETTE: (*Searching the SOLDIER's knapsack.*) He has nothing – no food – no matches – nothing – except, a letter.

FATHER: Who's it from?

BERNADETTE: (*Reading.*) His wife. She says she asked mayor's wife to write it...their son, Patrick, is dead...fever...she has no money, but the mayor's wife has given her shelter and...the rest is smudged... I should put it back –

FATHER: Nah! Keep it.

BERNADETTE: Why, father? It is his property, he should have it –

FATHER: I want it –

BERNADETTE: You can't read –

FATHER: No, I can't, but I can take it with me, go back to France 'n' find tha' lady. I can tell 'er 'ow 'er 'usband died smiling, thinking of 'er, perhaps. I can tell 'er 'ow 'e died quietly, without pain, 'n'...not alone...

BERNADETTE: (*Nodding and smiling.*) Then we shall, we shall, father.

FATHER: Yes – it's the right thing.
(*BERNADETTE moves over to her FATHER and kisses him.*)
Let's go – it's time.
(*The couple pack up their gear and exit. THE DEAD claim the dead SOLDIER, and lament.*)

Scene Three

A frozen road. THE DEAD litter the place, their lament distant, but audible. EUGENIE and GABRIELLE enter. They are both exhausted, hungry, cold, and dishevelled. EUGENIE in particular, seems dazed and delirious. GABRIELLE is trying to talk to her.

EUGENIE: Lace butterflies floating thus in my mind and swirling brash colours and love descends floating like whispers

GABRIELLE: Tha' may be, me dear, but 'onest to' say, you is gettin' on me tits with tha' rubbish –

EUGENIE: He sang to me in tones of yellow

GABRIELLE: Who's tha' then, love, yer 'usband?

EUGENIE: His eyes flashing...indescribable things

GABRIELLE: All me 'usband ever flashed me was 'is arse – dirty, 'airy thing – like a bleedin' shire 'orse, it was –

EUGENIE: (*She slumps to the ground.*) No more his aqua eyes touching this and that part of me...no more...

GABRIELLE: Come on, Jeanie, yer gotta get up, bleedin' miles to go yet. Come on, love –

EUGENIE: Piercing blue how I loved the mornings and the silence and the warmth

GABRIELLE: I'm tired of all this – I knows 'ow much yer loved the sod, alright? Bleedin' 'ell, woman, we's gotta get up 'n' go on – this is no place t' rest yer arse –

EUGENIE: Wrap me in colours of love and let eyes sing (*EUGENIE grabs GABRIELLE's arm.*) why did he hurt me why so much hurt like a hammer to a rose

GABRIELLE: Sod this! Yer sit there, then – freeze yer arse off! Fine with me, tha' is. Fine!

(*GABRIELLE moves away from the seated EUGENIE. Almost immediately, GABRIELLE spots a SOLDIER heating himself at a very meagre fire.*)

SOLDIER: Seen it before – that – seen it – give up, theys do – give up – sit down and fall asleep – only t'aint no sleep to wake from – that there particular sleep – no waking.

GABRIELLE: Thank ye for the advice, but she'll be just fine.

SOLDIER: All the same.

(*THE DEAD's lament is heard.*)

GABRIELLE: Wind is keen.

SOLDIER: T'aint no wind.

GABRIELLE: Nice fire.

SOLDIER: S'alright.

GABRIELLE: Difficult to get a fire going round 'ere.

SOLDIER: Like I said to a young man recently, 'Everything burns eventually'.

GABRIELLE: (*Moves closer.*) Yer wouldn't begrudge a lady from – (*Stops, horrified.*) Tha' be…is tha' a leg?

SOLDIER: It's the fat on the buttocks 'n' 'ips – tha's what makes it burn so well – fat – spit-spit fat bubbling – smells good 'n'all.

GABRIELLE: (*Despite herself.*) As…as I was sayin'…wouldn't mind, would yer…a brief sit down…just t' take the chill awa'…

SOLDIER: 'Always a price', said tha' too, 'always a price'.

GABRIELLE: We's got money, but no food – none at all.

SOLDIER: (*Getting up and moving toward EUGENIE.*) Is the lady cold, you think?

GABRIELLE: Think yer betta leave 'er alone –

SOLDIER: (*Squatting down besides EUGENIE.*) Nice face – pretty like – 'n' wha' a beautiful dress, me dear – yer could warm my 'eart –

GABRIELLE: I's said leave 'er alone –

SOLDIER: She's laughin', must mean she likes me – do yer like, love?

(*EUGENIE laughs and smiles at the SOLDIER.*)

Tha's right, yer definitely likes me, don't yer?

GABRIELLE: (*Trying to pull the SOLDIER away.*) Get off!

(*The SOLDIER pushes GABRIELLE away and launches himself at EUGENIE, groping and pawing at her. GABRIELLE produces her knife and stabs the SOLDIER in the back. The SOLDIER leaps up, screaming and cursing.*)

He attacks GABRIELLE and soon forces her to the floor, the knife spinning out of her hand. The SOLDIER beats GABRIELLE viciously. As if waking from a dream, EUGENIE realises what is happening, and slowly, stands up. Still in slow-motion, she walks to the knife, picks it up, returns, and stabs the SOLDIER again and again. The SOLDIER dies. A moment. GABRIELLE pushes the dead SOLDIER away from her and gets up.)

Good riddance to bad rubbish! Well, me lady, yer one of us, now. Shitting 'ell! The fire!

(GABRIELLE blows into the fire trying to keep it going, but fails, and the fire goes out. She stands and curses and kicks the dead SOLDIER. EUGENIE still stares at the dead man.)

Fuckin' Jesus! Fuckin' 'ell! All tha' for nothin'! Fuck!

EUGENIE: You...you let it go out?

GABRIELLE: Wha'? Yer...listen 'ere, it weren't my fuckin' fault, was it?

EUGENIE: You let the fire go out?

GABRIELLE: Wha' the fuck yer getting at?

EUGENIE: Typical really, everything you do gets messed up –

GABRIELLE: Withou' me yer'd be in –

EUGENIE: I should have lost you at the first chance –

GABRIELLE: 'N' I shoulda stolen yer money 'n' spat on yer body –

EUGENIE: Piece of pox-ridden scum –

GABRIELLE: At least I'm not daddy's whore –

(EUGENIE leaps at GABRIELLE with the knife. GABRIELLE steps back and EUGENIE falls, the knife falling out of harm's way. EUGENIE sobs. GABRIELLE stares down at her. Time.)

Gotta stick together me 'n' yer – oh yes, stick together.

(THE DEAD lament, EUGENIE cries, and GABRIELLE stares out into the wilderness.)

Scene Four

THE DEAD begin NEY's DEATH SPEECH, which echoes around the theatre, and once again uses lines taken from the play as a whole. NEY runs on stage, frantic. He looks wildly around and sees no escape. THE DEAD pick NEY up and manoeuvre him around the stage – one second he is upside down staring into the abyss, the next he rises upwards toward heaven, only to glimpse it before it is covered from his sight. NEY is both furious and terrified, occasionally trying to fight back.

THE DEAD: Thud-thud-thud-boom Moselle
    Another shot iron-hot Maastricht
    Head-hot boys-toys Wurzbourg
    Broken swords jagged-words Giesson
    Thud-thud-thud-boom Hohenlinden
    Hell-colours infused tones Elchingen
    Charging kaleidoscope-reds Jena
    Smells-sweat-sorrow-victory Magdeburg
    Thud-thud-thud-boom Eylau
    Hack-right slice-left Friedland
    Melting sight twisted sounds Busaco
    Boiling screams cold moans Smolensk
    Thud-thud-thud-boom Borodino
    Hateful-greens spiteful whites Lutzen
    Rag around discordant eyes Bautzen
    The final grey moaning skies Leipzig
    Thud-thud-thud-boom Quatre Bras
    And all fall down fall down fall down fall down
    (NEY is placed on his feet, dazed and disorientated. THE DEAD lament, scattered around the stage. Slowly, as if in a dream, BERNADETTE walks through THE DEAD, as if they were trees. She stumbles, falls, picks her self up and continues. Noises abound. She is scared, lost, and lonely. NEY tries to help her, but always is restricted by THE DEAD. Eventually she breaks free and falls to the ground. She shivers and moans. NEY stares at her. She becomes aware of him, and looks up, frightened. Sensing this NEY tries to reassure

her with a gesture, but BERNADETTE becomes agitated and looks for a way out.)

NEY: I…they…around us, even now and…**horror of penetration** –

BERNADETTE: Touch me – slice your head off –

NEY: They…infest us…as if…sharing space…infesting us…flee!

BERNADETTE: Twisted ankle – no excuse to come closer!

NEY: Do you…feel voices…

BERNADETTE: Feel?

NEY: Like water lapping…splish-splosh…

BERNADETTE: Ankle hurts –

NEY: **Can't punch rain**…ankle hurts…

BERNADETTE: Yes…

NEY: I could hack that ankle, rip it open, slice it in two, pound it, crush it, hammer it, blast it, smash it, mash it, flay the skin, melt the bones…but can't ease pain…

BERNADETTE: No… I thought not…

NEY: Cold?

BERNADETTE: Naturally…

NEY: *(Takes his greatcoat off.)* Take it…

(A silence whereupon BERNADETTE stares at NEY.) Please…

BERNADETTE: Can't walk…

(NEY walks over to BERNADETTE and puts the greatcoat over her shoulders. She flinches at his first touch, but allows the greatcoat to be put on. NEY sits besides her. He stares at her.)

NEY: Your face…as if a dream alive… I have seen you somewhere…sometime…

BERNADETTE: I am hungry…

(NEY takes off his shoulder-bag and gives it to her. He gets up.)

NEY: Giving…pity…the simplest act…no more relevant…as if emotion is redundant…how sad…

BERNADETTE: *(Seeing that NEY is leaving.)* Don't go… I…

NEY: Death-infested… I should not stay…please…live, do not die.

(*NEY exits. BERNADETTE opens the bag and looks into it. She looks up and stares after NEY. Her FATHER enters. He spots her and rushes over.*)

FATHER: I was worried – yer 'urt?

BERNADETTE: Ankle –

FATHER: Slow us down, tha' will.

BERNADETTE: No... I have to live...

FATHER: Nice coat... 'n' food...been visited by an angel?

BERNADETTE: Just eat – here – eat.

(*The FATHER eats. BERNADETTE stares after NEY. THE DEAD lament.*)

Scene Five

The stage is divided into three spaces. Stage right we see GABRIELLE and EUGENIE enter. GABRIELLE half-carries EUGENIE, who has clearly deteriorated in strength. Eventually, GABRIELLE sits EUGENIE down, and sits next to her. Stage left sees PILS bringing OUDINOT on. In an identical fashion, PILS places OUDINOT down and sits next to him. OUDINOT is still ill. Both sets of couples are obviously exhausted, undernourished, and suffering from the extreme weather.

PILS: No wood for fires –

GABRIELLE: No food for eating –

PILS: No shelter from the wind –

GABRIELLE: No rest from the snow –

PILS: We are dying –

GABRIELLE: We are fading –

TOGETHER: No solace in the maelstrom –

PILS: We should have stayed on the road –

GABRIELLE: We should have avoided the road –

PILS: We should have trusted others –

GABRIELLE: We should have trusted no one –

TOGETHER: We should have never come here –

PILS: Tell me something before you die –

GABRIELLE: Tell me something before you sleep –

PILS: What is it that plays on your mind –

GABRIELLE: What is it that drifts through your mind –
TOGETHER: Tell me a story of long ago –
OUDINOT: In the ballroom the lights sighed as stars –
EUGENIE: Colours drifted as midnight snow –
OUDINOT: And rainbow music caressed the air – tick –
EUGENIE: Eternal moments of forever –
OUDINOT: Tock –
EUGENIE: Searching for a glimpse –
OUDINOT: An identical purgatory –
EUGENIE: Tick –
OUDINOT: Of a million sluggish seconds –
EUGENIE: Tock –
TOGETHER: And then I saw –

> (*Both EUGENIE and OUDINOT get up and leave their scene. They walk timidly to stage centre, stop, and see each other as if for the first time. PILS takes over OUDINOT's lines, and GABRIELLE takes over EUGENIE's lines.*)

PILS: Such grace and fragility –
GABRIELLE: Such strength and majesty –
PILS: The world ground to a halt –
GABRIELLE: The world faded as haze –

> (*Very slowly, both OUDINOT and EUGENIE walk to each other across the space. They come to within touching distance, but stop and stare into one another's eyes.*)

PILS: And she came to me as murmur –
GABRIELLE: He stood shielding me with gentleness –
PILS: The light in her eyes drove away the blank moments –
GABRIELLE: His fragile might burned around me –

> (*EUGENIE slowly places her head on OUDINOT's chest.*)

PILS: The alive fragrance of her colours –
GABRIELLE: The air thickens beyond the reach of death –

> (*OUDINOT gently pulls EUGENIE's face upwards until they stare into one another's eyes.*)

PILS: Breathing our slightest gestures –
GABRIELLE: Haunted by our deepest fears –

> (*OUDINOT strokes EUGENIE's hair, and she in turn takes his hand and places it on her cheek.*)

PILS: The intricate glances of craving –

GABRIELLE: And our eyes knew each other –

> (*EUGENIE places her free hand on OUDINOT's shoulder, whilst he slips his free arm around her waist.*)

PILS: And out of silence is born the first star –

> (*EUGENIE and OUDINOT kiss and take leave of each other and return to their original positions.*)

GABRIELLE: Memories may warm us but feed us theys don't – we best get goin', miss, 'n' see if we's can find tha' man o' yours.

> (*GABRIELLE helps EUGENIE up and they drift off stage. At the same time, PILS grabs hold of OUDINOT and begins to strangle him. EUGENIE stops and looks round, but GABRIELLE gently leads her away. PILS climbs on top of the dying OUDINOT, but at once an OFFICER and two SOLDIERS enter.*)

OFFICER: Get him off! Get him off!

> (*The two SOLDIERS manage to wrestle PILS off OUDINOT, who lies panting. The OFFICER attends to OUDINOT.*)

Sire, I came as fast I could – when I saw him – are you hurt badly?

OUDINOT: (*Croaks.*) No…

OFFICER: Hold that man – we'll hang him at dawn –

OUDINOT: No…do not…

OFFICER: But, my lord, he –

OUDINOT: I said no…

OFFICER: Very well, sir –

PILS: (*As he is led off.*) This changes nothing – nothing – you hear – nothing!

Scene Six

The frozen road. TORZHOK staggers in slowly. He has deteriorated alarmingly and each step is an effort of sheer will power. He mumbles to himself, staring straight ahead. He stops and waits. ARNOUX enters. He is in an even worse state, and he shuffles along using his gun as a crutch of sorts. Every step in a torturous effort for him and it is no surprise that he collapses. Time.

TORZHOK: Been here before…seemingly…but white is white…dazzles…reflecting only ourselves…which is nothing…hah, Arnoux, we are wraiths of ghosts…shrinking…and the land grows…**inverse parallelism**…if I knew what that meant…been here before… (*Spots ARNOUX falling asleep.*) Oiy! Can't sleep, son… (*He goes to ARNOUX and kicks him until he stirs.*) Whilst it is true that we die a bit every time we sleep…here…we just die…no stopping…just stopped…do you understand you French fuck…my…my language disintegrates as fast as my body…interesting…don't you think…the body/language relationship…**obtuse parallelism**…obsessed with parallels…it's this road…each step expires me…like falling into a hole…when did we last eat…s'funny…not hungry any more…still, Paris…can't wait to get there…what do you think…a week…more…went to Brunswick once…my… that took two weeks…by coach…we won't make Paris…will we…still, keep trying…nothing else to do…that it should be reduced to this… the grand plan…the design… I wonder what she is doing now…right now…what time is it…at her toilet no doubt…regardless of time… time and the female species…grow apart…**mutually exclusive parallelism**…

ARNOUX: Torzhok……shut up…

TORZHOK: Try to stand, Arnoux…we have to be getting on…

ARNOUX: Nothing left…

TORZHOK: Maybe we'll rest a bit…can't harm…

ARNOUX: It is obvious…… I shall have……to shoot you……can't let you go…

TORZHOK: I understand…shall I sit…

(*Despite receiving no answer, TORZHOK sits next to ARNOUX. ARNOUX spends an age preparing his gun, but it is too heavy for him to lift. Gently, TORZHOK holds the muzzle to his head. Time. ARNOUX eventually manages to press the trigger, but the gun does not fire. Time.*)

S'funny...at the end of it...useless...these
things...useless...the fate of nations...yet useless...
(*ARNOUX slumps into despair.*)
Don't worry...we shall find one that works...perhaps we
should go now...it's getting on...night will come...like a
malevolent thing...with questions and whispers...

ARNOUX: Betrayed...each time...

TORZHOK: You have explained...and I respect that...that
your wife...with another did lay...a friend...it seems
discipline comes in many forms...

ARNOUX: Without discipline... I would fall apart...

TORZHOK: I had just thought of roses...how
marvellous...a theory: perhaps I am dead and just
dreaming of life...you should not have treated her
so...even mistakes have their truth...

ARNOUX: I couldn't treat her...any other...way...lies...lies
mutating...squirming inside like black-worms...

TORZHOK: Yes, my friend...lies...

ARNOUX: And I loved her...that's all...

TORZHOK: Still do...it doesn't drain away like pus...stays
to fester...love-infection

ARNOUX: And her dappled eyes...a palette of meaning...

TORZHOK: You are too sensitive to be a soldier...be a
poet –

ARNOUX: In the vacant moments... I dream of her...and
she touches this and that part of my soul...intricate
fragile gestures...like snow tumbling...

TORZHOK: More of that white stuff to come...we must go
soon... Paris paces this way and that...like a spoilt
child...

ARNOUX: Leave me......

TORZHOK: No...not now...

ARNOUX: I cannot walk...

TORZHOK: I can...

ARNOUX: Then...leave me...

TORZHOK: While it is true we walk alone...are thoughts
are multi-faceted...they demand your company...

ARNOUX: Leave me...

(Slowly, as if the effort is too much, TORZHOK gets up and picks ARNOUX up like a child. He shoulders his burden and walks off into the snow.)

Scene Seven

A checkpoint on the frozen road. Two SOLDIERS stand guard. GABRIELLE staggers on stage and spots the SOLDIERS.

GABRIELLE: Jeanie! Jeanie! Come quickly – we're here! Come quickly!
(The two SOLDIERS approach GABRIELLE and eye her suspiciously.)
Oh, thank the bleedin' gods – I could kiss the both of yer!

SOLDIER 1: You keep yer distance –

SOLDIER 2: Watcha doin' 'ere? Who are yer?

GABRIELLE: Gabrielle Arnoux, my stiff ram-rod gentlemen –

SOLDIER 1: Just wha' we need –

SOLDIER 2: Another loony –

GABRIELLE: Been marchin' for bleedin' days to get 'ere –

SOLDIER 1: Must be mad –

SOLDIER 2: Wha' for?

GABRIELLE: A secret mission – Jeanie –

SOLDIER 1: A secret mission?

SOLDIER 2: Better get the Captain –
(SOLDIER 1 exits.)

GABRIELLE: Look! Me friend's comin' – bit poorly she is – needs lookin' after –

SOLDIER 2: But not you, eh?

GABRIELLE: Strong as an ox, I is – but really, yer gotta 'elp the lass –

SOLDIER 2: Well, let's see wha' the captain's gonna say, eh?

SOLDIER 1: *(Entering.)* 'E says 'old 'er 'e'll be along shortly –

GABRIELLE: 'Old us?

SOLDIER 1: Look out – 'ere comes the other one!
(EUGENIE enters, worse for wear. GABRIELLE rushes to her and helps her.)

GABRIELLE: No worries now, darlin' we's 'ere 'n' these fine men is gonna 'elp us –

EUGENIE: Some water…

GABRIELLE: Come on, lads – yous 'eard the lady, give 'er some water –
(EUGENIE sits down aided by GABRIELLE who turns on the SOLDIERS.)
For Christ's sake – yer bleedin' bunch of bastards –

SOLDIER 1: Fuck yer, yer old dog –

GABRIELLE: Big man, eh? Screamin' abuse at shagged out women.

SOLDIER 2: *(Laughing.)* Watch 'er, man, big bitch with an attitude –

SOLDIER 1: 'N' a bigger pair of tits –
(GABRIELLE hits SOLDIER 1 on the jaw and he collapses. SOLDIER 2 jumps in and tries to hit GABRIELLE but she manages to defend herself. Before SOLDIER 1 can join in, the CAPTAIN enters.)

CAPTAIN: Just what in god's name is going on here?
(The SOLDIERS jump to attention. GABRIELLE stands ready to continue the fight if necessary.)

SOLDIER 1: These prisoners is fightin' back, sir –

CAPTAIN: Don't tell me you can't control two women, man, look at them!

GABRIELLE: Don't look like much, to be sure, but even so's gotta me dignity, love.

CAPTAIN: I can quite believe that, missus.
(The CAPTAIN walks past GABRIELLE and squats down besides EUGENIE.)
And whose clothes did you steal, me dear?
(The CAPTAIN brushes EUGENIE's hair away from her face and reacts.)
Holy ghost! The Duchesse de Reggio! Madame, allow me – you man, help me here!

(*SOLDIER 1 runs over and helps the CAPTAIN lift EUGENIE up. GABRIELLE tries to intervene but is held back by SOLDIER 2.*)

GABRIELLE: Leave her alone, you pig-fucks –

CAPTAIN: (*Picking EUGENIE up in his arms.*) Shut that whore up! Get her out of my way! Do it!

EUGENIE: (*Quite delirious.*) Stop ... My friend...my friend...

(*The CAPTIAN exits with EUGENIE as the two SOLDIERS beat GABRIELLE to the ground with their rifles. Eventually they stop, and follow the offstage order to 'hurry up'.*)

GABRIELLE: (*Sitting up, bloodied and dazed.*) Lost her again...lost her for sure...shouldn't be so hard...surely not...

(*GABRIELLE slumps, still sitting and the lights dim and we merge into another part of the frozen road. We see BERNADETTE and her FATHER. They lie still, the FATHER just awake.*)

FATHER: S'like blues...flashin' in me 'ead... 'n' skin veneer soft... I's bubblin' for yer, darlin'...can't arry 'em no more...pointless to ask... 'cause, darlin' look after 'er, yes, of course...

(*The FATHER sits up and looks at BERNADETTE. He strokes her hair and softly sings a lullaby to her. He produces a pistol and points it at her head.*)

It's alright, now... I mean...who'd thought tomorrow would be so extraordinary?

(*He tries to pull the trigger, but can't. He cries, throws the pistol away, and cuddles BERNADETTE.*)

No good...no good...

(*The FATHER huddles up to his daughter and sings again, only it doesn't last long, and soon it is quiet. NEY and NAPOLEON enter.*)

NEY: So......goodbye......

NAPOLEON: Ney – melodramatic now? You know, you're an old woman sometimes.

NEY: I don't like being abandoned –

NAPOLEON: Oh, really! Grow up! Me big chief – you little shit! Get it?

NEY: (*Turning away in anger.*) I'm sorry to have failed you, sire!

NAPOLEON: You and a million others –

NEY: (*Spots BERNADETTE.*) My greatcoat – look – it's her – the one I talked of –

NAPOLEON: (*Coming over and looking down.*) Ah, my pretty rose, Bernadette.

NEY: You know her?

NAPOLEON: Of course, Oudinot's bastard. It's what happens when you fuck some tart. Amazing that something so beautiful can come from something so horrid. Life: deliberately contrary.

NEY: (*Squatting besides BERNADETTE.*) What have we done?

NAPOLEON: We? Come, come, Ney, this is my moment –

NEY: (*Explodes in anger and grabs NAPOLEON.*) You fucking cunt! How can you be so – so –

NAPOLEON: They come Ney, say goodbye if you must.
(*NEY releases NAPOLEON and turns to see THE DEAD emerge from the gloom. They take BERNADETTE and her FATHER.*)
Two more to hate me...well, why not?

NEY: (*Horrified.*) Who...are they?

NAPOLEON: The price.
(*Time.*)
Come, Ney, the future stamps impatiently. Let us go.
(*NAPOLEON leads a reluctant NEY off stage. OUDINOT enters, leaning on a SOLDIER. PILS also enters, guarded by another SOLDIER. The CAPTAIN enters with EUGENIE, who seems to have recovered somewhat. EUGENIE and OUDINOT spot each other. Time. EUGENIE rushes to OUDINOT. They clasp one another.*)

EUGENIE: I thought...so many things –

OUDINOT: Eugenie, my love...so lost without you –

EUGENIE: And we walked and...such horror –

OUDINOT: Over now...together...

(*He pulls her away to look at her.*)

I said your name...every night...said your name –

EUGENIE: And I heard you –

OUDINOT: Prayed to be able to put it right –

EUGENIE: Hush now –

OUDINOT: Kept saying your name –

EUGENIE: And I am here –

OUDINOT: Sorrow – and –

EUGENIE: Hush now –

OUDINOT: Every night... I said your name –

EUGENIE: We shall go home now – and laugh with the future –

OUDINOT: Only by you did my heart always beat –

EUGENIE: Hush now...

OUDINOT: I don't understand...the things...if I could hold time in my hands...so different...so different –

EUGENIE: Time starts now...and forever more.

OUDINOT: You mean –

EUGENIE: Hush! Let us go home, we have a family to raise, remember?

OUDINOT: (*Completely stunned.*) I...

EUGENIE: (*Kissing him.*) Let us lose ourselves in each other...again.

(*They turn to go, but EUGENIE spots PILS.*)

Can this be...

(*She rushes to him and embraces him.*)

Brother, you have brought my husband home.

PILS: Aye, my lady, aye.

EUGENIE: You look so...all of you look so –

OUDINOT: The war, Eugenie, such horror. Pils, if you would help me, we have a long way to go.

PILS: (*Confused.*) But... I thought –

OUDINOT: What? The nightmare has gone, Pils, and no more will deceive us. Come.

(*OUDINOT holds out his hand to PILS who walks over to help him.*)

EUGENIE: No! I will allow no one, no one, to separate us again.

(*EUGENIE walks back to OUDINOT and helps him.*)
Let us go, gentlemen.
(*EUGENIE helps OUDINOT off stage, followed by PILS, the CAPTAIN, and the SOLDIERS. Time. TORZHOK enters carrying ARNOUX. GABRIELLE stirs and TORZHOK places ARNOUX across her lap, and sits down besides her. GABRIELLE stares at ARNOUX and TORZHOK, exhausted, talks.*)

TORZHOK: I saw the world frowning at me...yes indeed...frowning...snowflakes colliding...the desolation bellowing...even the mournful sky shrieks...no weight at all...none...they followed...oh, yes...respectful distance...very respectful...and though I tried still he slipped away and I begged and pleaded but still he slipped away and no weight at all none and still he slipped away and all I could do was watch him go...the simplest act...they have reduced us to savages and in our hollering we blurt out the sun......time enough...
(*TORZHOK stands and wanders off. The lights dim further. GABRIELLE holds ARNOUX and talks to him as THE DEAD enter, closing around her – some standing, some kneeling. They lament.*)

GABRIELLE: So many things unsaid oh yes unsaid and the world spins and tilts and the gaps and the possibilities and the wailing and the darkness but they have come Arnoux come from afar they are here Arnoux and they come with tears and farewells and love unsustained look Legrand smiling and cheeking Verdier who does not mind and loves him back there Merle sings his songs and Dulauloy throws his hat in the air and catches it again Corbinbau laughs at that and they clap each other's backs and Ledru and Razout pass the bottle and Marchand dances a jig and Foucher plays and plays till his heart will burst and Bruyere and Valence and Nansouty and Watther and Mountbrun and Delzons smile smiling yes smiling yes yes how they smile Arnoux my darling my darling

The End